Hope you enjoy reading this book Merissa. Lots of luck in future

Shyam x

Charlotte Greedy is a mum of two who is best known as @missgreedyshome. She creates relatable and funny content around her home and family life, as well as sharing what she's loving in the beauty, fashion, and lifestyle sector. She has also used her platform to raise money for mental health charities. She lives in Wales with her fiancée Harriet, her two children Enzo and Brody, and her fur babies Beau, Kobe and Minnie. *You Do You* is her first book.

www.penguin.co.uk

Charlotte Greedy

You Do You

bantam

TRANSWORLD PUBLISHERS

Penguin Random House, One Embassy Gardens,
8 Viaduct Gardens, London SW11 7BW
www.penguin.co.uk

Transworld is part of the Penguin Random House group of companies
whose addresses can be found at global.penguinrandomhouse.com

Penguin Random House UK

First published in Great Britain in 2023 by Bantam
an imprint of Transworld Publishers

A CIP catalogue record for this book
is available from the British Library.

ISBN 9781787636873

Typeset in Plantin MT by Couper Street Type Co.
Design by Couper Street Type Co.
Printed and bound by Clays Ltd, Elcograf S.p.A.

The authorized representative in the EEA is Penguin Random House Ireland,
Morrison Chambers, 32 Nassau Street, Dublin D02 YH68.

Penguin Random House is committed to a sustainable future
for our business, our readers and our planet. This book is made
from Forest Stewardship Council® certified paper.

www.greenpenguin.co.uk

FSC www.fsc.org MIX Paper from responsible sources FSC® C018179

For all the women who need to know they are enough as they are. Never settle for anything less than you deserve. xxx

Contents

Hello, You

Omigosh, hi! Thank you so much for opening my book. I really hope you're going to love it.

Maybe I'm doing this all backwards (classic Miss Greedy behaviour, haha!) but these are the things I want you to come away from this book knowing …

You ARE worthy.
You ARE special.
*You ARE loved **because of**, not in spite of, the stupid stuff you do.*
You CAN get your shit together.
YOU DO YOU!!

OK, this is a bit crazy, you've just opened MY BOOK?! I still can't believe it – I, little Miss Greedy, have written a book. A few years ago, I started an Instagram account to follow some home and cleaning accounts I liked and to post the DIY I was doing. I'd just moved into what was a pretty rundown and dirty council house and I was trying my best to make it into a lovely home for me and my two little boys, Enzo and Brody. I was living off barely anything back then so I was on a crazy tight budget. Such a small budget that my partner Harriet and I even made the boys a football goal out of old curtain poles – and they loved it!

I started getting some lovely messages from people who liked the projects I was doing and I thought, *oh my God! This is just amazing that people are even looking at my posts, let alone saying they like them and they want to try them out for themselves!* I look back on that now and I get goosebumps – I just can't get over how much has changed, to the point where I am now writing this book!

It was even more amazing because at that time in my life I wasn't in a very good place emotionally. I had not long come out of an eight-year relationship and I was a bit of a mess, to be honest. The positive feedback and lovely conversations I had with the kind and supportive people who followed me on my Instagram meant the world to me and gave me the confidence to turn the camera around on myself (admittedly, I'd had a couple of wines the first time!). I started to talk about some of the things that were more personal to me, like my struggles with my mental health, body image stuff, being a mum – and put up videos of me dancing around my bedroom like a tit while making my bed every morning (because don't forget, if you want to change the world, start off by making your bed!). Lots of people got in touch to say they had felt the same way at times and that seeing me talk about my experiences had meant a lot to them. If you've ever been in a dark place yourself and felt like you were the only one who felt that way, then you can imagine just how amazing hearing that was.

Don't forget, if you want to change the world, start off by making your bed!

In the time since I started @missgreedyshome, life has changed so much for me. Moving into that house in 2018 and making it mine, alongside all the support I got from my followers, gave me the fresh start I so badly needed. I still get lots of questions about all sort of things, from how I upcycled my kitchen to how I cope on days when my mental health is bad to how I got the confidence to put myself out there on Instagram, so I'm going to answer some of those questions here, in this book, but I also want to say a MASSIVE THANK-YOU to everyone who has cheered me on and encouraged me on my journey. I feel like I'm in the happiest, most confident place I have ever been in my whole life and I couldn't have done it without you.

I really believe that everyone deserves to get the life they want. That even when things feel like they are going to shit, you

CAN get a fresh start. Just because you feel a bit stuck, that doesn't mean your life is going to be like that for ever. The most important thing is that you don't have to live your life the way anyone else tells you to. There's a lot of pressure to act a certain way and that's really unfair. After all the stuff that's happened to me, I know that the only way to really be happy is to follow your dreams and be yourself. That's why You Do You. Those three words mean a lot to me. It's all about finding the confidence to do what you want – to live the way you want to live and not to please other people or because you think they're going to judge you. If you want to go and do something that no one else will like it doesn't matter. If it makes you happy, then go and do it.

You do you … I live by it.

The truth is that no matter what you do you are going to get judged anyway, so you might as well do what makes you happy, right? You are always going to get people who don't like you so they may as well not like the real you, rather than some version of you that you think they'll prefer! If you know authentically that you're happy that's the most important thing. Fuck everything else!

Nobody hands you a guidebook to life with all the right answers, yet there's lots of pressure on us to do things 'right'. But 'right' for you isn't going to be right for everyone. So many people stress

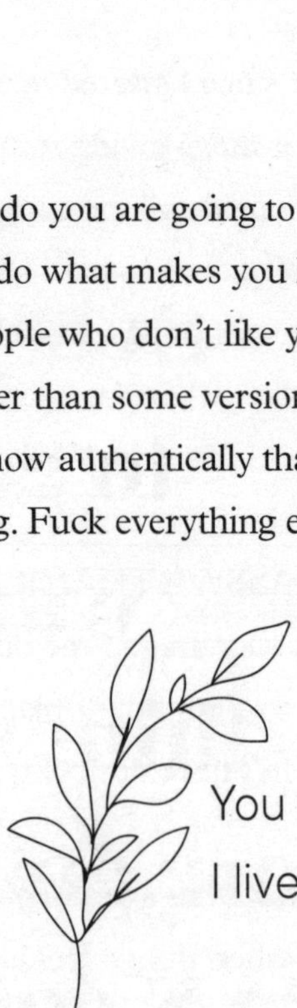

You do you …
I live by it.

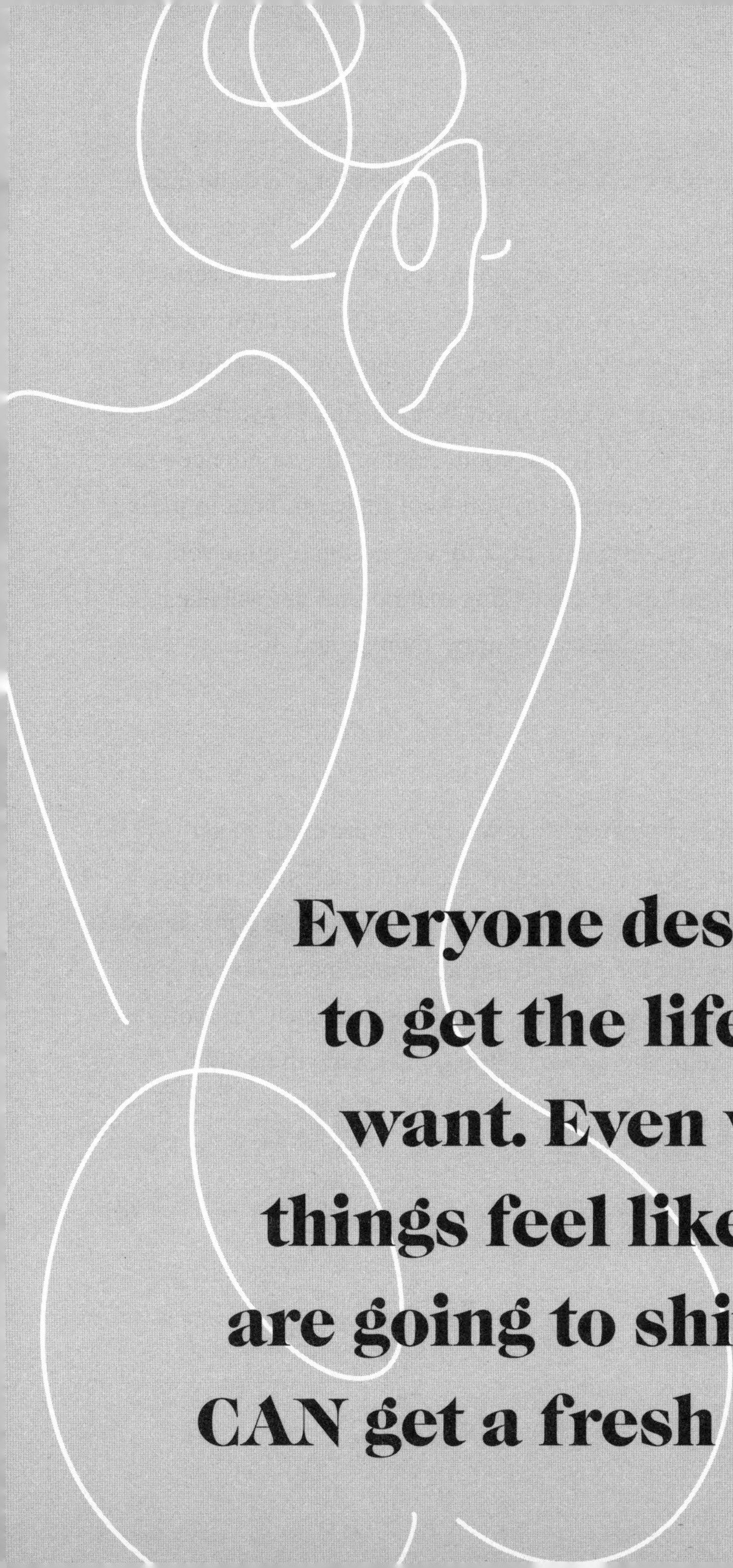

Everyone deserves to get the life they want. Even when things feel like they are going to shit, you CAN get a fresh start.

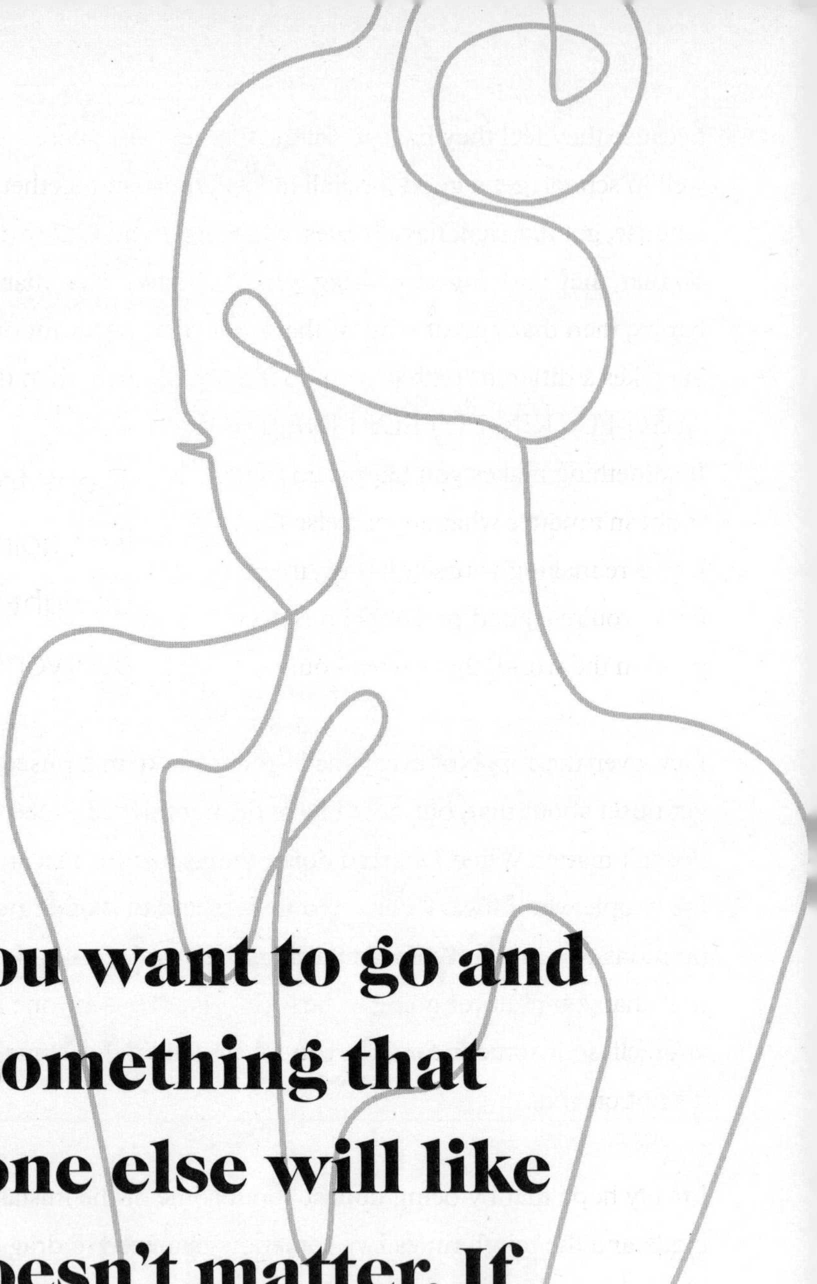

If you want to go and do something that no one else will like it doesn't matter. If it makes you happy, then go and do it.

because they feel they have to follow this set path in life – do well in school, get a good job, fall in love, move in together, buy a house, get married, have babies, whatever – and if they don't do that, they're doing something wrong. If that's what makes you happy, then that's great – but if that's not what you want or your life takes a different path or you do it all backwards, then that's ABSO-FUCKIN-LUTELY FINE, TOO!

If something makes you happy, go for it. It doesn't matter what anyone else thinks. If you're making yourself happy, if you know you're a good person who is doing good in the world, that's what counts.

'Right' for you isn't going to be right for everyone.

I am over-the-top. Not everyone is going to like me. I used to get upset about that, but now I have the confidence to see that it doesn't matter. When I started doing things just for me, and for the people who I love, I started to understand that other people's opinions of you don't mean anything. What it all comes down to is that you're never going to be – you *can't* be – anyone but yourself, so if someone judges you for that, then that's on them, it's not on you.

I really hope that by being honest about some of the mistakes I've made and the tough times I've somehow managed to drag myself through it might help you, too. If you feel like you're in a hole and you don't know how to get out of it, maybe some of the things that have worked for me will work for you, too.

I would love it if by the end of this book you feel like you don't have to compare yourself to anyone else, you just have to figure out what makes YOU happy and go for it.

We are all different, and I know my story isn't yours, but I really hope that in sharing some of the life lessons I've learned (sometimes the really bloody hard way!) it might help just a bit.

I definitely haven't followed a conventional life path and I know that at various points, lots of people wrote me off and thought I wouldn't amount to anything. And sometimes I believed that and it really knocked my confidence, but at the same time I'm stubborn and I always wanted to do the opposite of what people expect of me. Which can make me a pain in the arse, it's true, but it's also given me the determination to get through some really shit situations that I think could have crushed me otherwise.

I got in trouble A LOT at school. I was a clever kid, but sitting still and learning maths and English really wasn't for me. I got kicked out of school and didn't do my exams. And I didn't have the best relationship with my parents growing up. I was a hard kid to raise and I think they didn't know what to do with me, so they mostly just shouted at me instead. Then I found myself in a relationship. I was ob-SESSED. I'm sure you've been there, too. They suddenly become the most amazing person ever and you're so lucky that they even notice you. I'd do whatever they said without question.

It took me a long time – way too long – to figure out that feeling like this did *not* make it a good relationship. People can be very controlling and sometimes it feels like you have to do whatever they want. Cook, clean, lend them money to go away with their ex-girlfriend while you stay at home … (Yeah, I know, I can't believe I fell for that either.).

But although relationships can be toxic and I have gone through stages where I have been really angry, that's the thing about life: we all make mistakes (and God knows I've made loads) and shit things do happen – but they are what make you, you. Without them, you'd be someone completely different. You can't paint over your past.

Miss Greedy's Home was the start of getting the life I wanted. I had a safe place, a home that was just mine and the boys'. Sure, I was broke and the house was in a real mess at first, but I cracked on with finding creative and cheap ways to transform the house and make it look exactly how I wanted it. And the feedback I got from all the lovely people online made so much difference and really spurred me on. Then I got together with my amazing girlfriend Harriet, who is an absolute superwoman.

That first year after I started @missgreedyshome was so tough, but figuring out a way to decorate my home on a budget and posting about it kept my mind busy even when I sometimes felt like I was drowning. I didn't always know how to solve the big problems, but I kept putting one foot in front of the other, working towards making a home for the three of us, and slowly things got better. The Insta-friends I made who I spoke to daily, who laughed at my videos of me dancing around with an umbrella on my head or wearing an inflatable sumo suit and sent nice messages, kept me sane (as sane as it's possible for me to get!) and I kept going somehow. As I transformed our house from the rundown, dirty state that it was when we moved in (complete with cigarette ends and worse everywhere) to a home that I was proud to bring up my boys in, I transformed, too.

You can't paint over your past.

One day, I wrote a post about how I thought that everyone deserves a fresh start and that we all CAN change things if we want to. I got a huge response from people who felt the same way. It turns out everyone's been through their own shit and really just needs to hear from someone else at that moment. So, if you've picked up this book because you feel like you're struggling then I really hope you'll find some of the things I've written about in these pages helpful. Believe you have the power to get the life that's right for you, that makes you happy. Know that I'm rooting for you and you deserve the absolute world.

Sometimes it's not about changing your life at all, though. You may not even realize that your life is perfectly fine as it is, it's just that you've been told that it's not. Or maybe you've convinced yourself it's not because you're looking at what everyone else is doing and think that you're supposed to have the same things as them, even when you know on some level that it's not right for you. I promise you that you don't. The most important thing in the world is to keep believing in yourself and working on finding the things that make you – YOU AND NO ONE ELSE – happy, then you will get there. Remember, it's your life. YOU DO YOU.

We all CAN
change things
if we want to.

I haven't always been strong and I haven't always been motivated, and even now I still have bad days when I have a hard time doing anything at all. As you'll know if you follow me on Insta, I have borderline personality disorder (BPD) and there's no getting around that as it does affect my life. Even though I'm in the best place I have been in my whole life there are still days when I feel sad and shit, but I have found coping mechanisms that I'm going to tell you about. Obviously what works for me won't work for everyone, but it's worth trying. The point is to try.

It's taken me a long time to get to where I am today – in a good place with two happy, amazing kids, a partner who loves and respects me, a safe and comfortable home and a job I love. I'm going to tell you about how I did it and the things that have worked for me, in the hope that you'll find lots to recognize and maybe take away and try out yourself. With some belly laughs along the way! But more than anything, I want to inspire you,

You CAN
get the life
you want.

you beautiful human reading this, to figure out what you want, what makes you happy and to realize that you CAN get the life you want. Which, now I've written that down, sounds like a really big ambition! But I'm going to do my best.

Because that's all any of us can do, right?
Our absolute fucking best.

Make Your Own Rules

We all feel so much pressure at every age to do what everyone else is doing. When you're an adult, that might be to buy a car, get a mortgage, buy a nice house. And to find a partner (with sometimes rigid ideas of what sort of person that should be) and to have a baby. When you're a child or a young person, that might be to get good grades, go to uni and/or find a good job. I really believe that the most important thing at any age is to know how to tell the difference between what you want and what other people and society expect from you. And to find the courage to act on that. It's hard to know what will make you happy if the voice inside that tells you is being drowned out by the opinions of everyone around you.

We all feel so much pressure at every age to do what everyone else is doing.

That pressure starts when you're a kid. The message you get at school is that the most important thing in the world is to get all the right exam results. Whether you are academic or not, that's what you're told you *have* to do.

I don't know about you, but when I was young it felt like there was one way to do well and to succeed and if you didn't match up, then there was something wrong with you. At least now there is more recognition of mental health struggles and conditions that affect learning and behaviour like ADHD (attention deficit hyperactivity disorder) and Asperger's than there was when I was at school, but kids can still be put in the 'naughty' or 'good' box, or the 'clever' or 'stupid' box. That affects not only how they are treated by teachers but what they come to expect for themselves.

♥ The 'naughty' kid ♥

My childhood and teenage years were a bit of a rollercoaster! To be fair to my parents, I was hard work and could be very difficult to deal with. And to be fair to me, they did an absolutely terrible job of it at times. It probably didn't help that my sister, Danielle, who is just eighteen months older than me, was a studious, academic, obedient child, who always did everything that was

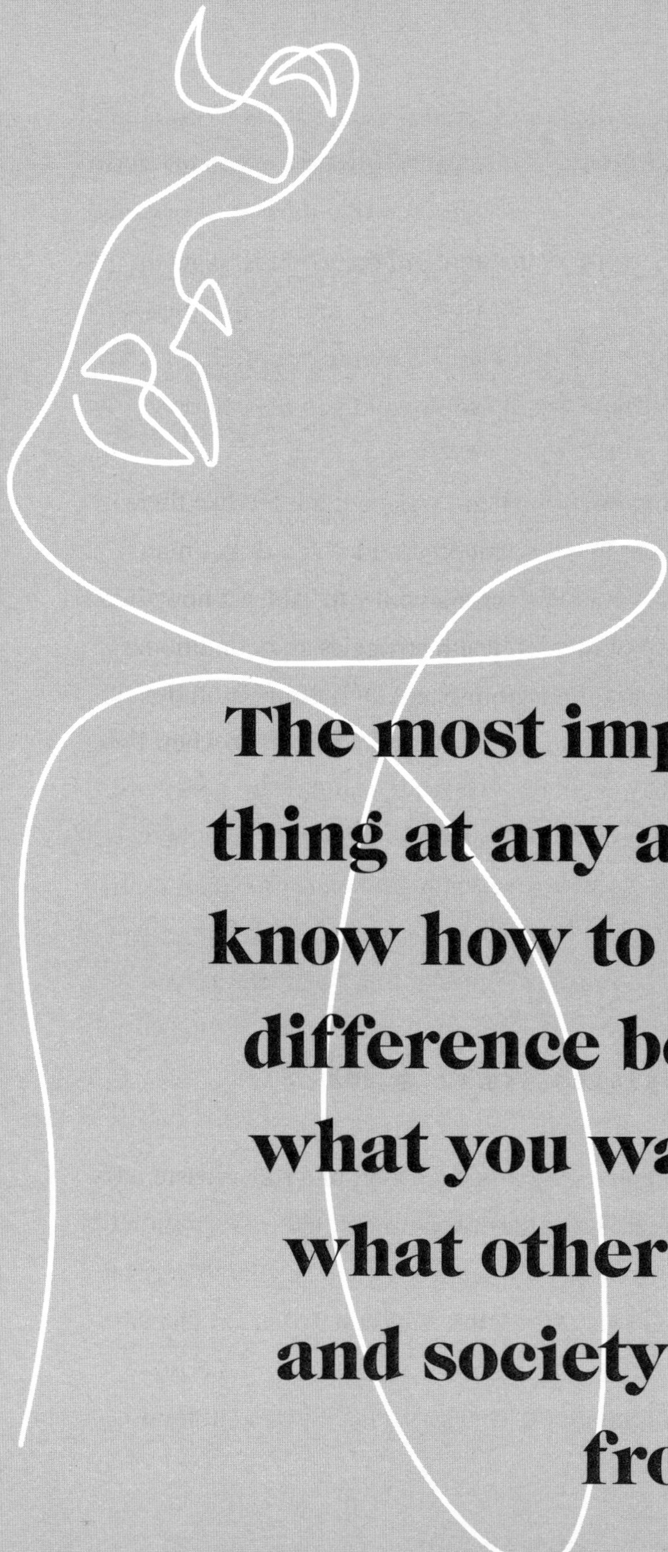

The most important thing at any age is to know how to tell the difference between what you want and what other people and society expect from you.

expected of her. And then they had me, who definitely didn't! They couldn't understand that we were different; they must have thought if one kid could knuckle down, work hard and do as she was told, then why couldn't the other?

It's so easy to forget what it's like

It's so easy to forget what it's like to be a kid. I really think that it's an important feeling to hold onto – even though a lot of us would probably prefer to forget most of it! But it's the best way to connect with and understand what the young people in your life are going through. Adults can look at a kid who gets into fights and doesn't do what they are told and decide they're just a naughty kid, but they are often the most sensitive and they act out because they don't know how to deal with how they are feeling. And then this affects what kind of adult they become. I bottled everything up and it made me into an even bigger mess. I can see now that I was trying to put that wall up so things wouldn't hurt me so much – 'Shout at me, I don't care.' And then you take that into your adult life because you learned all the wrong ways to deal with how you're feeling.

I was really stubborn, too, and I didn't like authority. Which was just one more reason why I clashed with my dad, who was a strict disciplinarian. It was still the era when a lot of people thought it was fine to smack kids, so if I did something wrong I'd be sent to my room with a slap. I was always on report at school and I'd panic when I had to go home to my parents and tell them I was in trouble again. I knew that I was going to get shouted at. I couldn't talk to them about what was going on in my head and because I was often in trouble, they always assumed that everything that happened was totally my fault. But that's not how it works with kids, is it? When they get into fights with other children, for example, it's often more complicated than that.

I was always the loud kid who got into trouble. I think the issues started when I was in Year 3. The earliest time I can remember was when our teacher was off and we had a supply teacher instead. He was lovely, but for some reason I didn't like him. We were supposed to be writing things down, but at the end of the hour he saw my page was blank. He asked me why and I didn't say anything. 'I'm speaking to you,' he said. But I wouldn't reply so he went into the next room to get another teacher. When I still wouldn't reply, she said, 'GET UP.' I didn't so she picked me up and took me to the cloakroom and threw me. Literally threw me. I hit my head on a peg. She shut the cloakroom door and went to get the headteacher. By the time the headteacher had come I had lost my shit and was punching the walls. The headteacher calmed me down, contacted my parents and said, 'There's been an incident.' I don't know if they thought I had probably deserved it, but from their reaction I got that they thought it was OK that the teacher had picked me up and thrown me. In fact, my parents were so angry with me that when I went back into school the next day I wrote the teacher a letter saying 'I'm really sorry'. When I look back now, I'm fuming that I went back to an adult who dealt with the situation wrong and I apologized.

I was diagnosed with ADHD when I was in Year 8. My mum and dad took me to this place where they assess kids with behavioural problems, but they didn't explain to me what was happening or why I was there. I remember sitting there thinking, *what the fuck's going on?* I had to do all these different tests, like an X came on a screen and I had to press a button. I didn't get what the doctor was saying to me. For a start, he had a strong accent that, as a child, I couldn't understand and I was too scared to say. The problem was that I had so many walls up by then that I couldn't tell anyone how I felt or that I didn't understand. I didn't say a thing in any of the sessions I had with this doctor.

After a certain number of times going there I was told that I had to take these tablets, which were Ritalin, which is a classic prescription for ADHD. But I wouldn't. It was never explained to me what was happening and how these tablets might help me, it was just like everyone wanted me to take them to make their lives easier because I was such a nightmare. It wasn't ever presented to me in a positive light, like it was OK and the tablets were potentially a good thing for me (which I now think they might well have been). I refused to accept there was something wrong with me even if everyone else seemed to think there was, though I do think I knew deep down I wasn't like all my friends and my sister. The Ritalin just became one more thing in the constant battle with my parents – I wouldn't accept anything they said could be right and they wouldn't listen to or try to understand anything I said either.

Getting kicked out

My Catholic secondary school, which was the sort of place where they wanted you to always have your tie on straight, couldn't deal with me and for some reason they thought it would be a good idea to send me two days a week to this 'naughty school' for kids who caused trouble. But this place was insane: you could literally do anything and they'd just let you get on with it. My memory of it is that if a fight got too bad they'd call the police, but that was about it. So predictably, that made me worse, because on the days when I was back at my Catholic school I just thought, *well, I can throw a computer at my other school, so if I lose my rag here I'm going to do that here and you can't stop me.*

My Catholic school didn't want to expel me as it would have made it hard to enrol me anywhere else, so they advised my mum and dad to take me out voluntarily to make it easier for me to be placed in another school. My parents put me in a school closer to where we lived, a local area where the kids were harder. The toughest girl in the school didn't like me – the boys were coming up to me saying she had broken people's noses and she was going to come after me. I pretended I didn't care but on the inside I was shitting myself.

We were in the canteen one day and I could just feel that something was about to kick off. Some of her mates, who were bullies themselves, pushed me into her. She said I'd barged into her and started trying to dare me to fight her. My survival instinct kicked in. I thought, *I can't let her know I'm scared.* And I completely lost it. I screamed in her face and started punching the metal shutters that closed off the counter from the rest of the canteen all around her head. Then I went into psycho mode and the teachers couldn't control me. It was pretty bad, but the girl walked away and didn't bother me again. There was no way I was getting my nose broken – haha!

I learned a really important lesson that day, though. The situation and being targeted by those girls made me realize that although I'd never thought of myself as being as bad as that bully, I had been a bully at my old school and I did used to say nasty things to the quiet kids, though I wouldn't have had the guts to do so to the bigger kids. I'd stood up for my sister against someone who was constantly goading her at my old school – and she could have killed me too, she was like a bull! But I didn't think at the time that I was doing exactly the same thing when I said horrible stuff to other girls who didn't have a sister or a friend ballsy enough to stand up to me. It took that bully at my new school to make me grow up a bit and realize I didn't want to be like her, that definitely changed me for the better.

When I was at school I could be a right twat to other kids and I really regret that. I was miserable at home and I didn't understand or like myself at that age so I took it out on the people around me. I was going through my own stuff, but it was still a horrible thing to do. At least I was a kid who grew up and grew out of it – some adults don't and they are still bullies. It still makes me really sad to think that some of the stuff I said to some of the quieter kids probably marked them and I am truly sorry for it. If my kids were horrible to anyone like that I'd be really upset.

I really believe that all the things that happen to you shape who you are. You can't undo any of them and they all got you to the point where you are today, so what else can you do but find a way to accept them and learn from them? For example, the way I was parented has massively affected how I bring up my kids because I know how important it is to listen to them and not just shout at them or assume it's all their fault if they get into trouble at school. At the same time, though, it's important to acknowledge the stuff that didn't go right and to admit it if you've acted like a bellend. It doesn't make me a bad person as I was just a kid, but I do regret the way things turned out at my school. It was a good place and there were some good teachers there who had tried with me and wanted me to stay. So that was a massive life lesson for me. I don't have a close friendship group from school like lots of people do and I got kicked out of my other school in the end, so I didn't do prom nights or any of that end-of-school stuff where you celebrate with your friends. I stayed in touch with some of the girls from my Catholic school, but they stuck together from when

At the same time, though, it's important to acknowledge the stuff that didn't go right and to admit it if you've acted like a bellend.

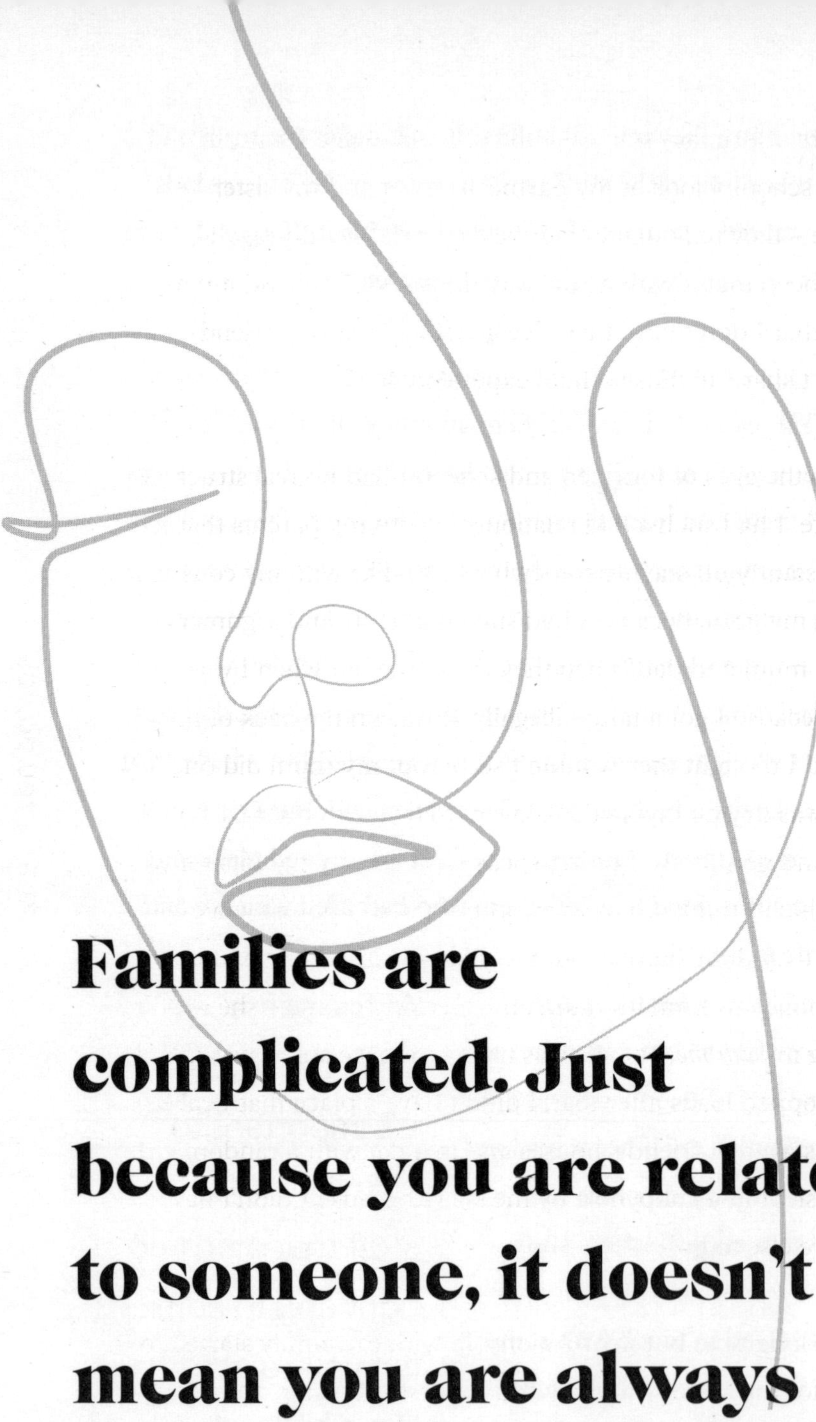

Families are complicated. Just because you are related to someone, it doesn't mean you are always going to see eye to eye.

they were at primary school, some of them, while I was off at another school. I look at my partner Harriet and my sister Danielle – they're going to their best friends' weddings who they've been mates with all the way through school and it makes me sad that I don't have that. I've got some amazing friends, but we didn't share all those school experiences.

Between the ages of fourteen and sixteen I had no real structure in my life. I had such a bad relationship with my parents that I was constantly off staying somewhere else, like with my cousin or Grandy, my gran, because I had such big fights and arguments with my mum and dad. Then they threw me out when I was fifteen because I got a tattoo illegally. It was on the back of my neck and I thought they wouldn't see it, but my mum did one day when I was drying my hair. So I went to live with my best friend Emma and her family. I didn't speak to or see my parents for a while, which I think did us the world of good. Though while I thought they didn't care about me, I later learned that Mum was giving money to Emma's mum and checking on me – she wasn't checking in *with me*, but she was trying to make sure I was OK. I house-hopped loads after that, I didn't have a place that I called home. I stayed at friends' houses and in a flat with a random girl, where I slept in a cubbyhole by the stairs because I didn't have anywhere else to go.

It took a long time but my relationship with my family started to change for the better when my son Enzo was born in 2013. I got a lot closer to my mum again and my sister Danielle came round all the time because she was besotted with him. Now I cook for my parents when they come to see the boys and my dad is a really good grandad to them as well as an important male figure in their lives. He's a better grandad than he was a dad in lots of ways and that's had a positive impact on my relationship with him. I've gained a lot of respect for him after watching him with my two sons over the years. Enzo's latest thing is that he wants to grow a top knot, like the footballers. He managed to get the tiniest bit of hair into a ponytail the other day and was really proud of it. My dad was round and tried to tell him that long hair is just for girls but Enzo just laughed at him. When I was young, that was the sort of conversation that would have quickly turned into a row. It was great to see that Enzo can love his grandad but not be bothered by my dad's completely outdated views.

The truth is that families are complicated. Just because you are related to someone, it doesn't mean you are always going to see eye to eye with them. But at the same time, it can be hard to completely ignore what your family thinks, even when you don't agree and it doesn't reflect your values. But that's just a fact of life and something we all have to learn to navigate as we grow up and figure out who we are and what's most important to us, away from what anyone else thinks. But what I can see now that I'm nearly thirty is that even if you don't have a good relationship with your family at a certain time in your life it doesn't mean that won't change in the future and bridges can't be mended. My parents are never going to change who they are and I'm not going to change who I am to try to get their approval, but we

Bridges can be mended.

have found a way to get along OK most of the time and I'm really happy that they are a part of mine and Enzo and Brody's lives.

Finding your way

My mum told me recently that she'd had a conversation with my auntie when I was younger that she thought I wouldn't see my eighteenth birthday. I understand why she thought that. By the time I was fifteen, before I moved out, my mental health was terrible and I was drinking a lot and self-harming badly. I was doing crazy diets and not looking after myself. I was writing in my diary how I wanted to kill myself and my mum read it one day.

At this time in my life, when everything was already going to shit at home, there was someone in my life who I looked up to as a sort of father figure, who took advantage of my vulnerability. I started to feel uncomfortable with the way he hugged and kissed me and then a few things happened that made me realize that this relationship was weird and that what he was doing was wrong. It gave me the creeps and I started trying to avoid him. It went on for about six months and I didn't know what to do because I had no one I felt I could talk to about it. Because

> Looking back, my stubbornness definitely got me into trouble, but it also got me through.

I had anger issues and behaviour issues I thought I'd be branded a liar if I ever tried to speak out about it. Kids who are like what I was like back then so often don't get believed so I self-harmed because I was really struggling and didn't know what to do.

So yeah, I was such a mess at this point in my life. I think what got me through in a weird way was that I was so bloody stubborn! On some level, I knew I wanted to prove everyone wrong; whatever anyone expected of me, I wanted to do the opposite. Looking back, my stubbornness definitely got me into trouble, but it also got me through. When my dad said I would never amount to anything if I didn't get good grades, deep inside a bit of me was always like, *I will. I will prove you wrong.*

I'm definitely not saying this is the best way to go about your life (being stubborn is not my most appealing character trait, even if it has proved useful at times!), but I would say to anybody that just because someone has certain expectations of you – whether they are good or bad – that doesn't mean they are right. It takes a while to figure out for most people, it's true, but only you can define who you are and what you're capable of. (And I promise you, you are capable of so much more than you think.) My sister Danielle was always the golden child and she's done everything by the book. She went to uni, then straight into a good job at twenty-one and now she has a nice house, a fiancé and a gorgeous little girl called Robyn. And I have a job I love, my own house, an amazing partner and two gorgeous little boys who are the absolute world to me. We are completely different people who

Only you can
define who you
are and what
you're capable of.
(And I promise you,
you are capable of
so much more
than you think.)

have lived completely different lives, but we have ended up in similar places despite what people expected.

❀ If you're a teenager ❀ now ...

When you're at school, it can feel like you have to be the smartest, the most popular, someone people fancy, or it's a massive disaster. But you don't, and it's not how it is. First of all, you aren't going to be stuck there for ever. There's a big wide world out there and although that can feel scary, it means that school isn't the be-all and end-all. All you can do is try your best and take the opportunities that are offered to you, but if the academic route isn't for you, then don't worry about it. If you are really excited about going to uni, then good for you. But if you're not sure that's what you want to do, then there are lots of other things you can do instead. There is more than one path available, you just have to find yours. Just because everyone else is doing something doesn't mean you have to do it as well. Look around and see what sort of life other people who are maybe a bit older than you have if it inspires you or helps you to figure out how to get the life you want.

There's a big wide world out there,

There is more than one path available, you just have to find yours.

But don't fall into the trap of comparing yourself to others because you can only be you.

Everything can feel like a mad rush when you're in your teens, but you do have time. You don't have to do absolutely everything at once and you don't need to know all the answers yet. And actually, that's true even when you're older. If there is some magic age you hit and you suddenly know what you're doing and how to be the perfect adult then please let me know because I definitely haven't got there yet!

Whatever age you are, but particularly when you're young, when you have a big decision to make, if you can, take some time to think about what you're good at, what you enjoy and what you want your life to be. If you're still living at home or you're lucky enough to have some job flexibility, then this might be easier. Whether it's about education, deciding to take a job, moving in with someone, moving to a different place, just giving yourself a week or two to mull over a decision and work out if you're doing it for you or because other people expect it of you could really help.

You don't need to know all the answers yet.

Love whoever you love

Figuring out relationships, sex and who you fancy is of course another big part of growing up and our early experiences often have an effect on what we think and feel when we're older. Everyone was in such a rush to have sex when I was younger. No one wanted to be the last one to lose their virginity. But I think that's really shit if you have sex for the first time because you think you have to, because all your friends are doing it. And yet there is so much peer pressure and expectation that it can be so hard to do your own thing and not be influenced by everyone else. It breaks my heart that young people, mainly girls but not just girls, are doing things sexually that they are not really ready for yet because they think they have to. Sex is meant to be a way of connecting with someone that's fun and exciting, but it's not going to be if you're doing it for the wrong reasons.

> Sex is meant to be a way of connecting with someone that's fun and exciting, but it's not going to be if you're doing it for the wrong reasons.

I was such a late developer. My friends were all off snogging their boyfriends at break and lunchtime and all I would let my boyfriend do was hold my hand (bless him!). They called me 'fridge', short for frigid! I remember we went on a school trip in Year 7 or 8 for a couple of days. The boys had to sleep down one end of the hostel and the girls were at the other end and I didn't even get why! Then one night, all of us girls snuck over to the boys' corridor so we could see our boyfriends. I wasn't that bothered about seeing mine, especially when I discovered there was a drinks-can crushing machine on the wall, which for some reason I thought was brilliant, and I just stood there while my friends were all snogging their boyfriends. Completely oblivious, I was living my absolute best life crushing cans! (*Goes on Amazon, looking for wall-mounted can-crusher.*)

When I was younger, I didn't know anyone who was gay. Except for possibly two of our teachers, as the rumour was they were lesbians. (I think every school had two female teachers who everyone said were a couple. I wonder if they still do?) I was really drawn to one of them. I couldn't put my finger on why, but looking back, I obviously had a crush on her, although I didn't recognize it as that at the time! She wore sportswear and looked like a stereotypical butch lesbian. Come to think about it, Harriet is her doppelgänger! I've basically ended up with my childhood crush (though H is much better-looking. Winning). And actually, there are people I went to school with who I now know are gay. Things have got better as there are so many more gay and trans people visible in public life, but it's not perfect and

If only there had been more lesbian celebrities and just out people in life that I was aware of, it would have helped me to understand myself.

you still hear kids using 'gay' as an insult, which is such a shame. If only there had been more lesbian celebrities and just out people in life that I was aware of, it would have helped me to understand myself. I don't think I even knew what a lesbian was – it was only that the boys were saying it about our teachers.

One of the things I find hardest to respond to on social media are the messages I get from young people asking me how they should 'come out' to their parents. I didn't have a relationship with my mum and dad so it wouldn't have occurred to me to tell them anything, let alone about how I was feeling or who I liked. So it's not something I feel like I can give any advice on. My parents found out because someone told my sister I'd been seen kissing a girl and she told them. My dad sent me a message saying, 'Get home now!' Which obviously I ignored and went to stay at my friend's house instead. Because we didn't get on, and they never talked to us about sex or relationships or anything like that, I just wouldn't have talked to my parents about it.

And also, to be honest, I really don't like the term 'come out'. I can see that if you are close to your family you might want to talk to them about it, which is great, but to me, 'come out' implies that being straight is the 'norm' and it's on you to make a big announcement to the world if you don't fancy people of the opposite gender. You're supposed

To me, 'come out' implies that being straight is the 'norm'.

Who you fancy, your sexuality, is an important part of who you are, sure. But it's not everything about you.

to go to your parents and say, 'Mum, just for you to know, I'm gay.' Why can't a girl just come home and say, 'This is my girlfriend, Patricia', or a boy say, 'This is Derek, my boyfriend'? And their parents would just be like, 'Oh, hiya. Nice to meet you.' If you come home with someone you love and you want to introduce them to your family, then that's the news, isn't it? Not whether they have a willy or a vagina. Why does it matter?

Who you fancy, your sexuality, is an important part of who you are, sure. But it's not everything about you. And anyone who doesn't accept any part of who you are can do one. That's on them, not on you. You don't have to play by anyone else's rules or feel sad if they don't approve. If you want to tell anyone in your life about which gender you think you're going to be sleeping with, then go for it. But equally, I don't think you should have to. Just snog who you want to snog. I know things have changed so much even in the time I have been an adult, but it would be nice to think that in a few years' time, there won't be all this and no one will have an opinion on the gender of the person you fall in love with.

Just snog who you want to snog.

About two years ago, Enzo asked why he's not got a dad. I was expecting it, obviously, so it wasn't something that took me by surprise. I said, 'Well, you've got two mummies. Some people have two daddies, some people have a mum and a dad. Some have only got a daddy or a mummy. Some haven't even got parents; they have grandparents or another adult who looks

So long as kids feel safe and have people who love them, you can see that they take pretty much any set-up in their stride.

after them.' He seemed totally unbothered and he's never asked since, and Brody's never asked. It did surprise me a bit that it is the only question I've been asked by my kids – though they haven't learned yet about how babies are made, so there might be more to come! They just don't seem to notice or care. Probably because they know other kids who have two mummies or two daddies.

There's every kind of family combination under the sun now, and how unbothered kids are when they haven't been subjected to the old-fashioned prejudices that some adults have just proves what a lot of bullshit those views are. It's not even just about being gay or straight. My friend has a kid from a previous relationship and so does her partner and they have a kid together so it's a proper blended family. Each one of the kids has a different set of biological parents but it doesn't matter, because they are surrounded by adults who love them. That's normal these days and so long as kids feel safe and have people who love them, you can see that they take pretty much any set-up in their stride. This is just another area in which a load of old-fashioned and outdated beliefs still influence what people say and think, even when those views don't help anyone.

Brody is just as likely to come home from school and tell me about his boyfriend as he is about his girlfriend. I love that my kids are growing up in a world less prejudiced than the one I grew up in,

I love that my kids are growing up in a world less prejudiced than the one I grew up in.

and so much better than how it was for previous generations. I really hope that they and the kids that come after them grow up knowing that they are free to love whoever they love without anyone judging them for it.

Being there

My kids aren't teenagers yet (technically, that is. Some days it feels like Enzo's not far off!) so I can't tell anyone how to parent a young person (also, when I say 'parent', I obviously mean anyone who has a parental role). But I do remember what it was like and I think that's the key: we all need to try to remember how it felt to be a teenager and see it from their point of view if we're going to do a good job of supporting them. I really think that they've got it harder than any of us. They've been through a pandemic for one, plus they're growing up at a time when everything is so uncertain … and expensive. Just look at the ridiculous price of houses! Kids are constantly being measured, assessed and graded at school, which is exhausting. How would you like it now if several times a day someone gave you a mark for how well you did something? 'I'm going to give you a B for talking to that customer because you were mostly polite but a C for wiping down the draining board because you missed a bit.' I'd tell them to piss off!

And do you remember how fast stuff happened at that age? It feels like a long time when you're in it, but between the ages of fifteen and eighteen a lot of kids do their GCSEs, decide about college, A levels or an apprenticeship, have sex for the first time, get a part-time job, often learn to drive, maybe pick a degree and fill in a massive uni application … It's mad when you look at it like that. Plus, they're full of hormones and rowing with friends and breaking up with and getting back together with boyfriends and girlfriends. That's a lot.

Don't get me wrong, I'm terrified of Enzo and Brody going off into the world where I can no longer protect them. A part of me hopes that they will always live right round the corner. (I actually have a plan here – I'm going to try to take them on holiday all over the world so they get so bored of travelling, they never want to go anywhere ever again. Boom!) But I know there will come a time when it's not as simple as me telling them to do their homework or brush their teeth any more – they'll have to make their own decisions. All I'll be able to do is support them. In the meantime, I want them to be kids for as long as possible. To do their best and hopefully do well at whatever they try, but not to feel so much pressure to succeed that it takes something away from their childhood.

We need to talk

This is something I have had to learn in the last few years. I could never have written this book even a couple of years ago because

I always struggled to express how I felt – I bottled everything up until it came rushing out uncontrollably and I'd lose my rag. My parents never came down to my level and asked me why I had done something, how I felt or even praised me. Which wasn't great, admittedly, but it has shown me how important these things are, which has in turn made me a much better parent.

My sons remind me of me and my sister. Enzo is mostly good at school and loves his maths and English, while Brody gets into trouble but has this brilliant imagination. To watch him as his little brain comes up with ideas when he draws and plays is amazing.

When Brody comes home and he's been naughty he tells us. He's a kid with a temper, just like I was (er, still am sometimes!) and he's got to learn to manage that. But I know from my own experience that if I blow my lid and punish him he won't learn. We don't sugar-coat it or ignore his bad behaviour, but I think you've always got to end a negative with a positive. So Harriet and I will go through what happened and make sure Brody understands what he's done wrong but also make sure we understand why he did it. And we'll always talk about the things he did do well, too, and give him something to work towards. I never want him to go to his room and cry by himself like I did, I want him to cry to me so I can help him be better. I have to be careful not to be too soft on him because I see myself in him, I do know that. As

You've always got to end a negative with a positive.

Harriet said, 'Sometimes you have to tell him off but not then immediately give him a chocolate biscuit, Charl.' Haha! Fair enough, I can see she might have a point there.

Shouting doesn't work

I'm going to give myself some advice here now, because I know I'm not a thinker. I am sometimes bad at taking a step back and not reacting instantly. (Harriet is the opposite. She's a bloody saint. She never loses her shit or says things she doesn't mean in the heat of the moment, like I do.) But I was a kid who was shouted at and I know it doesn't achieve anything.

I was a kid who was shouted at and I know it doesn't achieve anything.

I remember pushing my mum and dad's buttons so I need to try to remember what I used to do because it can keep some of the more annoying things the kids do in perspective. For example, when my boys are laughing and messing about in the back of the car it annoys me so much that I could literally headbutt the windscreen. But they are doing it because they're just kids and they're bored, so they'll start laughing and poking each other. So as much as on the inside I'm yelling, 'Would you two just shut the fuck up?!', I have to remind myself that I used to do the same thing. If Enzo moves and kicks my seat just once I'll tell him, 'Stop kicking my seat!!' But I used to do it to my mum all the time – and on purpose!

Every adult shouts sometimes. You're not a bad person if you're tired and you lose it occasionally, but we all have to try really hard to make sure it's not about the big stuff. The more you have a go at kids, especially if they already know they've done something wrong and they need you to help them find a way to be better, then you're chipping away at their confidence and showing them they can't come to you.

If you've got a kid who's naughty, who is running away or gets into fights, then there is a reason. And if you as a parent can get a good relationship with them then it's much more likely you'll be able to get it out of them. I think we all know really that shouting doesn't work. If you're a hot-headed parent (trust me, as someone who is one!) and you go in there all guns blazing, then most likely it will mean your kids will slowly put up a wall between you. They'll think, just like I did with my parents, *I can't talk to them because I'll get yelled at.* And once that wall is up, you're not going to get it down easily or quickly.

It's so, so hard when you're tired and frustrated, and we all have those moments when we just don't know what to do. I try my best to always remember that I'm the adult and to take a step backwards before I react. What's the reason they're acting like this? Are they struggling and they don't know how to come to you?

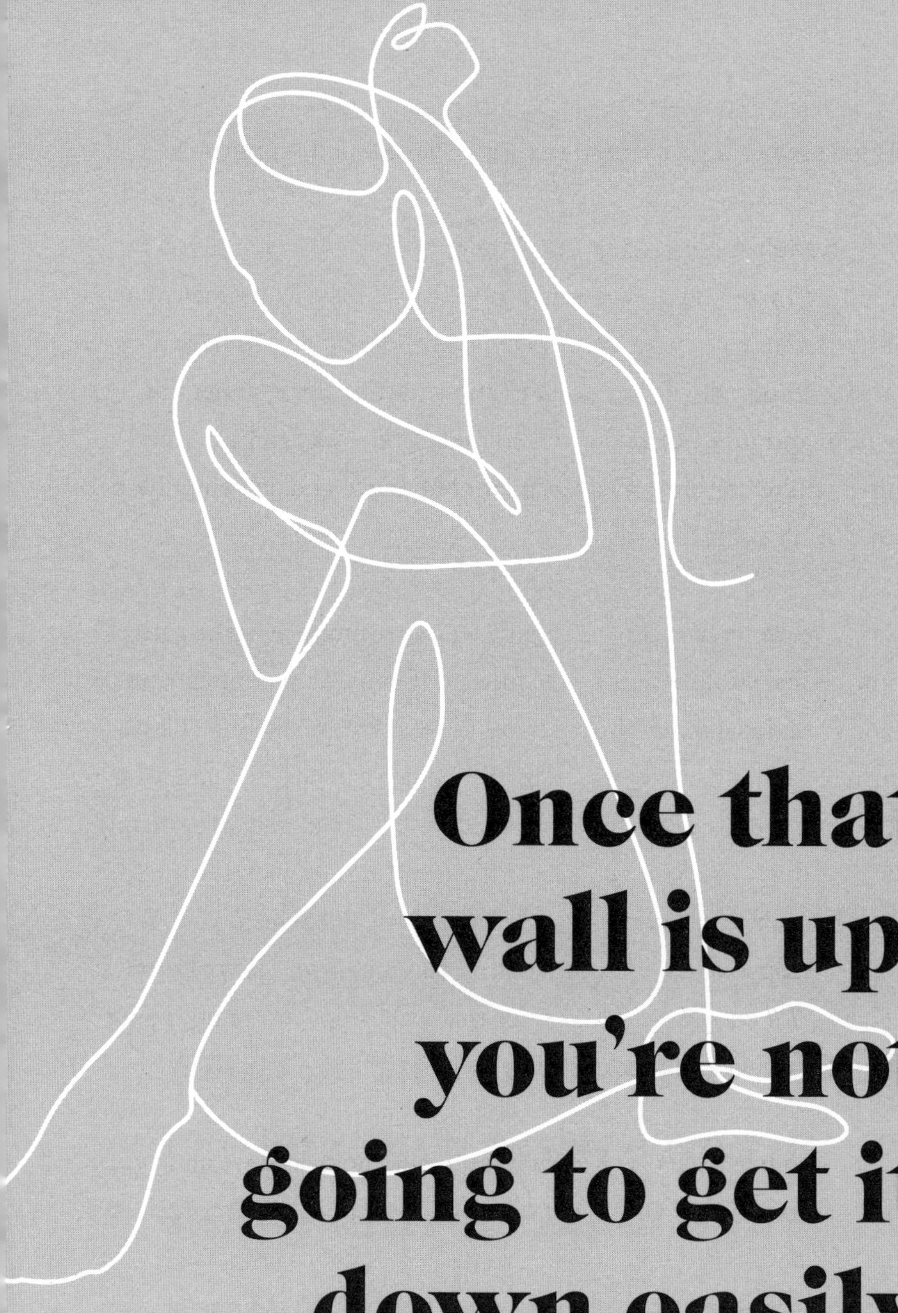

Once that wall is up, you're not going to get it down easily or quickly.

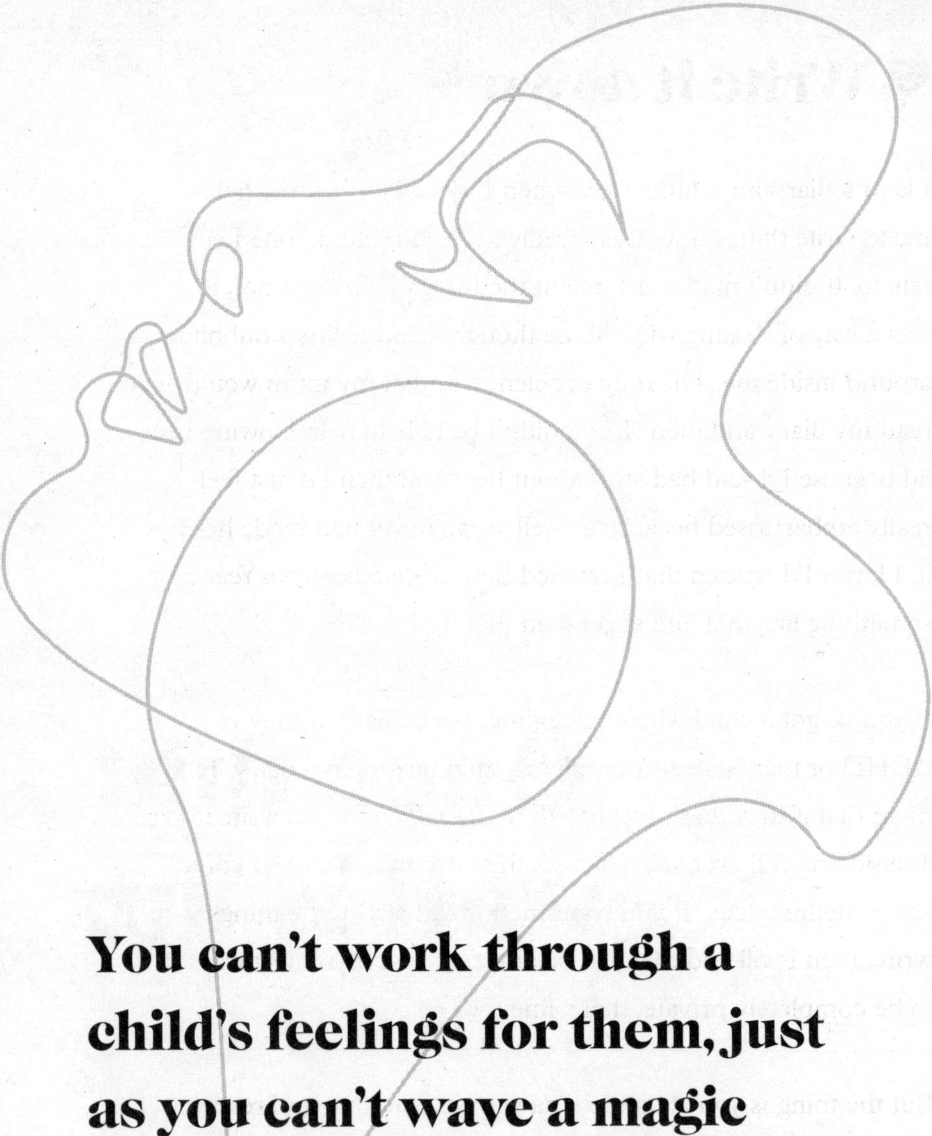

You can't work through a child's feelings for them, just as you can't wave a magic wand and make anything that might hurt them disappear. Just be there ready to support them when they need you to.

♥ Write it down ♥

I kept a diary for a little while when I was a kid. It really helped me to write things down, especially as I felt I had no one I could talk to. It didn't matter if I meant the things I wrote or not, it was a way of dealing with all the thoughts and feelings bubbling around inside me. The only problem was that my mum would read my diary and then she wouldn't be able to help blowing her lid because I'd said bad stuff about her. And then I'd just feel really embarrassed because as well as whatever had made her lose it, I knew I'd written that I fancied Samuel Jenkins from Year 6 or something like that and she'd read that too!

If you've got a child who's struggling, particularly if they've got ADHD or mental health problems, then buy them a diary. Tell them that if they don't feel like they can talk, they can write it here and no one will ever see it, unless they want them to. You could say something like, 'If you want me to read any of the things you write, then I will and that will be amazing, but if you just want it to be completely private, that's fine too.'

But the thing is you absolutely have to stick to that and respect their privacy. I know it might be hard if you're worried about them and want to know what's going on, but you just can't read their diary. If you've got a child who wants to write in a book privately, then you have to let them do that or they won't trust you. Plus, they might just need to get stuff out and be a bit dramatic, and you don't need to know about that. If you read that they've written 'I hate my mum and I want my mum to die', then you're understandably going to be really upset, but it's probably just them needing to get something out of their system in that moment. They won't mean it. But reading it could change your relationship with them in a way it's hard to come back from. You can't work through a child's feelings for them, just as you can't wave a magic wand and make anything that might hurt them disappear. As they get older, you have to give them increasingly more space to work through their feelings and just be there ready to support them when they need you to.

Children's brains are full just like adults', but they don't have the right techniques to deal with it all yet so I think a diary is a brilliant idea for a young person who's finding it hard to deal with their emotions. And starting a diary when you're young means you get into a really good habit that may be really helpful as an adult, too. Whatever age you are, it's always only going to be a good thing to give yourself time and space to work out how you feel about something, what you want, what is making you happy or unhappy … isn't it?

Find out what YOU want and go for it

I couldn't follow the rules that other people set for me. The structures of school didn't work for me and I was written off as a naughty child. I have to take some responsibility for that, but I still think that these narrow ideas of what it means to be successful get embedded into us as kids and then carry on messing with our heads as adults.

I couldn't follow the rules that other people set for me.

It's so easy to forget what it was like to be young, but we need to do our best to remember because it means we have more compassion for ourselves now and makes it more likely that we can connect with any young people in our lives – whether that's our kids, our friends' kids, our grandkids, our younger siblings …

It can take a lot of hard work to get where you want to be in life, particularly if you have big dreams.

But that's exciting, provided you are working towards the right things. So I think we have to let our kids be kids and take the pressure off if they're not academic, or if it takes them a bit longer to do something than it does their peers. You don't need to be the one everyone fancies, or wants to be mates with, or who has the best job or the nicest house to be happy. You just need to give yourself the space and time to figure out what YOU want and go for that, without feeling you have to explain yourself or apologize to anyone for that.

Give yourself the space and time to figure out what YOU want and go for that.

If you've got great predicted grades and everyone expects you to go to uni but you want to go travelling for a while and have the money to do that, then great, do that. You can always apply another year. Or not. If all your friends are getting jobs in offices but the thought of sitting behind a desk all day makes you feel sick, then listen to that. What would you like to do instead?

If everyone keeps asking you when you're having kids but you don't think you want a family, then that's absolutely fine. Don't create another human being just because your mum keeps telling you she wants to be a grandma.

If it feels like everyone else is doing one thing but the thought of that feels wrong, then always listen to that voice. Maybe you'll want to do it in the future. Maybe you never will. But trust your instincts.

That's the only way to make your own rules and build a life that's really yours.

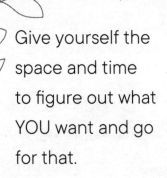

Love Is Love

I've been together with my amazing, wonderful Harriet, who many of you will know as 'H', for four years now. It's taken meeting Harriet and building a life based on love, mutual respect, support and always having a laugh together to make me properly realize what I wanted, and what I deserved.

Every single person is different and when we get together with someone how that relationship works (or doesn't) is always going to be unique. Only you can decide if you're with the right person. I'm going to tell you about what I've learned from going from a relationship that made me feel terrible to one that has made me happier than I thought possible, in case it helps you, even in just a small

Only you can decide if you're with the right person.

way. There is so much I wish I'd known when I was younger, but then again, that's the problem with being young, isn't it? There's so much you don't know and sometimes you end up learning the hard way …

The first thing I want to say, though, is that I really hope you don't recognize anything from your own relationship in me and my history. But if you do, just know that you deserve so much more. You are strong enough to get out, if that's what you need to do, and you are worthy of someone who respects you and treats you well. There are organizations offering free support (*see also* page 62).

What love isn't

I was still a girl when I had my first proper relationship. We lived together almost from the beginning and she took over my world completely. I first caught sight of her when she walked into my local pub. I thought she was the most exciting person I'd ever met. I'd never been with anyone before, though I pretended I'd slept with loads of people because I thought it would make me look cool. My friends were off shagging boys when we were that age and I'd never been interested, but I didn't know why. When I saw her something just clicked in my brain.

When you're young, you think love is meant to be dramatic and passionate, don't you? I didn't know anything about being in an adult relationship and so I went along with so much stuff because I was in awe of her and I didn't know any different.

With her, I felt like I always had to look a certain way. I had to look girly and to dress up when we went out. Nowadays, I don't wear make-up very often and I tend to wear gym clothes a lot, but I would never have left the house dressed like that when I was with my ex because I didn't think she'd like it. I thought that if her ex-girlfriend was a proper housewife who cooked and cleaned for her then there was an expectation for me to do the same. I didn't have a clue how to cook, but I figured it out because I wanted to impress her. It was like a lesbian version of your 1950s man-about-the-house and dutiful wife stereotype in a way!

I used to think she might check my phone and my social media messages. So I would delete all my message threads with my friends, which made me feel guilty, like I was trying to hide something even though I wasn't doing anything wrong. As the relationship went on, we used to have the worst rows. I thought I couldn't leave her because I'd never cope on my own. I didn't know that wasn't how it was meant to be, that good relationships

Good relationships are about mutual respect and trust, about lifting someone up.

are about mutual respect and trust, about lifting someone up and not feeling so shit that you think you aren't enough by yourself.

I'm not blaming everything on her. I think that's important – to recognize and reflect on when you've behaved badly too. She knew I had a temper and how to get a rise out of me. She used to call me a psycho. I once got so angry with her that I threw a mirror down the stairs, which was stupid and dangerous. Enzo has seen a lot of bad rows and I really wish he hadn't. That breaks my heart now. I did some stupid stuff when I was in that relationship and I was definitely a cock at times, but that doesn't make me a bad person. Actually, recognizing when I was at fault too makes me a stronger, better person.

When I was twenty, we decided to have a baby. I was so young and I didn't feel I was ready, but I went along with it. We were arguing a lot and like a lot of people, I stupidly thought starting a family would solve our problems. And I worried she would leave me if I said no. Which are really *not* great reasons for deciding to have a child, I know now! I'm so lucky that I had Enzo as he has completely changed my life, helped me grow up and saved me from being someone I didn't want to be. But I'm also aware that it could have gone another way – I could have got post-natal depression, for example, and struggled to cope, what with the situation I was in. Social services had been involved in my own childhood and I never wanted to get into that position as a mother myself. And fortunately, I didn't. I love being a mum and my boys are by far and away the best thing to have come out of

I'm so lucky that I had Enzo as he has completely changed my life, helped me grow up and saved me from being someone I didn't want to be.

I love being a mum and my boys are by far and away the best thing to have come out of that period of my life.

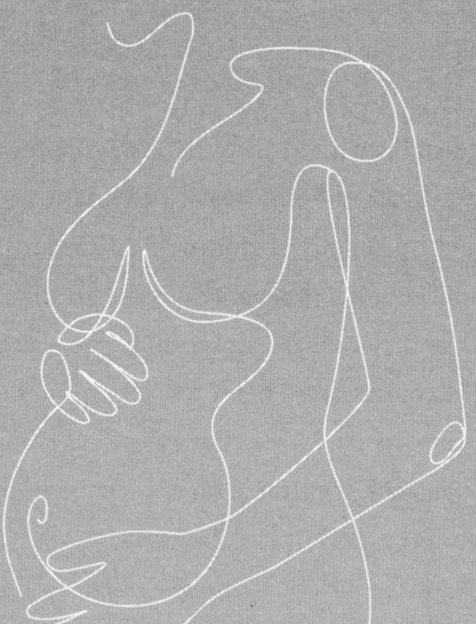

that period of my life. It also helped heal some of the problems between me and my own mum because she came over and helped out a lot. I'm so grateful that Enzo and Brody are happy, well-adjusted kids, despite some of the things they've seen.

When I was pregnant I was really anxious and the birth was traumatic. Then, when Enzo was just a few days old, my ex took him to her sister's without me. I was alone in the house, bawling my eyes out. It felt like that was a way of showing me that she could take him away from me. I was scarred and for many months after I wouldn't let anyone else babysit him. Not even my mum.

❀ Getting out ❀

Things started to change when I was pregnant with Brody. It was partly because I wasn't a little girl any more, I was a woman. I wasn't comfortable with some of my ex's friendships with her peers and I was stuck at home heavily pregnant and looking after Enzo. A massive turning point for me was Bonfire Night, 2015. I was nearly eight months pregnant and had arranged with my ex to take Enzo to the fireworks in Pontypridd. She was going to meet me there, but I couldn't find her. I was dragging the pram across a muddy field and trying to look after Enzo. I was in pain and ended up sitting in the pram with Enzo on my lap, texting her 'Where are you?' over and over. It wasn't until right at the very end of the night that I found her. It was then that I realized I just couldn't take her shit any more. I just couldn't believe that we were having another child in a matter of weeks, yet I never seemed able to get hold of her. I was nearly done with the relationship and maybe she could see that, because things did change a bit after that. I think on some level she knew I wasn't totally under her spell any more. I knew things weren't right and I didn't want to stay with her, but I worried that if we broke up, I would only get the kids half the time – and I wasn't prepared to leave her and not be with my kids. Because I had issues with my mental health and had been diagnosed with borderline personality disorder, I was scared that I wouldn't get custody. Of course I now know that's not true.

The end of any relationship is difficult. Even if you both agree that it's time to go your separate ways, it can be hard to adjust to life without that person and it can take courage to face being on your own again if you've got used to having someone around, even if you know they aren't right for you. I know my situation was extreme, but all I can say is that you CAN do it and, in my opinion, it's better than looking back and regretting that you settled for something that made you unhappy.

When you are in a controlling relationship, ending it is so much harder. People who are manipulative and seek to control will often try to isolate you from friends and family who would usually be there to offer you support. Most of my friends at the time were mutual friends so it was hard to talk to them about the relationship, how I felt or what I needed.

You CAN do it.

It can take courage to face being on your own again.

Luckily, my best friend Emma was there for me and supported me so much. We'd drifted apart a bit because she didn't get on with my ex and so I'd stopped seeing her as often, but then I started seeing her all the time again. Brody and her little boy are the same age, so we had that in common, too. She knew what our relationship was like, but she didn't have the full picture of everything that was going on. I started to open up to her a bit more and she made me realize I could leave if I wanted to. She helped me understand some of what I went through. And I'm glad to say that, although we went through a terrible time, my ex and I are in a better place now. We have managed to work through our issues and are both in our kids' lives.

If you ever find yourself in a situation where you need help, please know that it's OK to ask for it. If you're in a relationship that has battered your self-confidence, then seeing a way out can seem almost impossible without good people around you to help, practically and emotionally. There are organizations offering free support and advice (*see also* page 62).

Harriet – my H

I know you guys think that my story with Harriet – or 'H' as I usually call her – is some big fairy tale (I mean, it is now!), but it didn't start like that. This is the story of what actually happened …

H and I grew up and lived in the same street when I was about four. We played netball together for the same club during our school years and we were Facebook friends, but beyond that we hadn't ever known each other well. I'd always fancied her and I had a suspicion that she was gay but was told she had a boyfriend.

Then, towards the end of my relationship with my ex, at a time when I was feeling lost and lonely, I'd seen on Instagram that H was recovering from a serious back op. She'd posted a photo of her and her mother – who I thought was her girlfriend! When I realized later in the day that it was actually her mum, I messaged her on Instagram to say that I hoped she was recovering OK and to tell her I'd mistaken her mum for her girlfriend! (I was basically fishing to see if she was gay, obviously.) We started talking. I remember thinking, *oh my God, she is DEFINITELY flirting with me!* but I was still with my ex and so it could only ever be a friendship. We started to meet up for lunch sometimes but always with my best friend Emma. All three of us became really good friends and H started to find out more from Emma about the toxic relationship I was in – Emma could see the chemistry between us and knew from the get-go that H was perfect for me.

I did start to fall for H while I was with my ex. I'm honest about that, even though I'm not proud of it. But sometimes it takes that. I think sometimes you meet the right person at the wrong time and if you're meant to be with someone, you're meant to be with them. There's a saying I love: 'I believe that true love meets you in your mess, and not your best'. Everything about H showed me

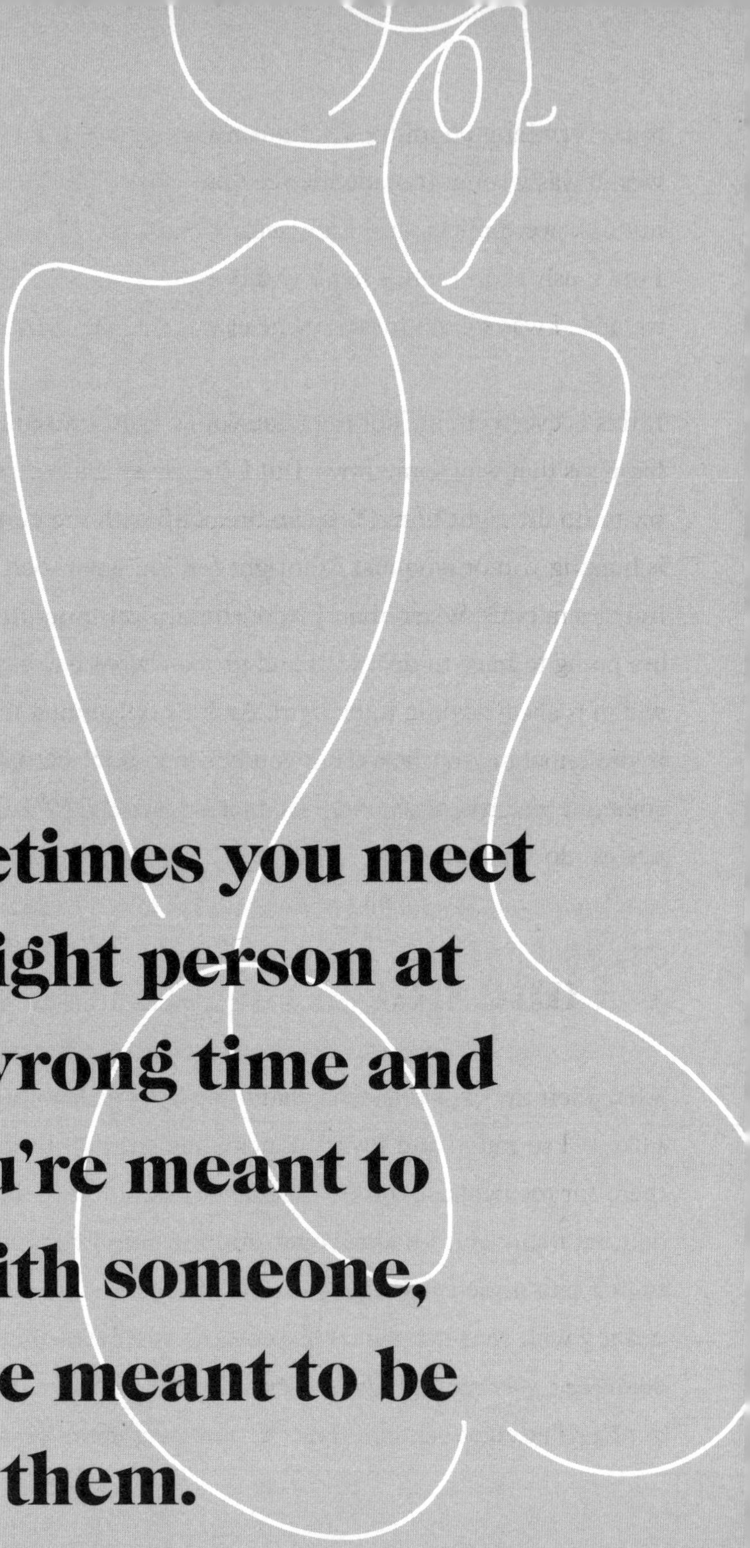

Sometimes you meet the right person at the wrong time and if you're meant to be with someone, you're meant to be with them.

that everything about the relationship I was in was wrong. It made me see that not only were my ex and I not getting on, I obviously didn't fancy her any more because I was falling for someone else.

Try to do the right thing.

If this is ever you, try not to blame yourself. Because life just happens that way sometimes. But I'd also say that you should try to do the right thing. You can break up with the person who is hurting you or who just isn't right for you – you don't have to hurt them back. When that relationship is done and dusted, you are going to have to deal with and process what has happened, which is always going to be hard. And it's only going to be harder if you know in your heart that you behaved badly, too. Whatever someone else has done you have to ask yourself, 'What sort of person do I want to be?'

Time out

After I left my ex, I realized I had to be by myself for a while. I liked H so much and I was so lucky that she and Emma were there for me because there's no chance I could have done it without them. But I had to focus on Enzo and Brody and I had to prove to myself that I could stand on my own two feet. I was dealing with so much shit at the end of my relationship and I could so easily have gone downhill, but it was my responsibility not to. I had to show myself, my ex and everyone around me

It's not OK if someone ...

- Regularly criticizes you and makes you feel embarrassed.
- Controls or tries to control what you do, what you wear or your money.
- Tries to cut you off from your friends and family.
- Acts like everything is your fault or makes out that you're crazy.
- Wants to check your phone all the time and control who you speak to.
- Puts pressure on you to have sex or do anything sexual that you're not comfortable with.

If you need help and support, and particularly if you are afraid, there are people who can help. In the UK, look up: www.womensaid.org.uk/information-support/ Or call the National Domestic Abuse freephone helpline twenty-four hours a day: 0808 2000 247.

If you are a victim of abuse and need immediate help, lots of chemists and even other places like banks and supermarkets operate a 'Safe Spaces' scheme. Look out for the 'Ask for ANI' logo. This stands for 'Action Needed Immediately' and there will be staff there who are trained to help you call the police and get help discreetly. Please don't forget that abuse isn't always physical, coercive control is now a crime too.

that I'd made the right decision and that I could cope. That's my stubborn streak again, doing the opposite of what everyone expects me to! I had to get a good life for the three of us and make us a home.

Getting straight into another relationship without taking some time out would have been a mistake. For all I knew, I might have been drawn to H because I was comforted by her, because she was the first person who I'd liked apart from my ex. I had to prove to myself this wasn't the case, and also that I wasn't simply leaving my ex for H. It was about seven months before H and I got together officially, though she was still a huge part of my life before that.

I had to get a good life for the three of us and make us a home.

It was the right thing to do. We all know that when we're going through a lot we generally aren't in the right headspace to make decisions. And I really believe that when you've been in a relationship that has shat on your self-confidence, you need to build that back up for yourself. It can only come from remembering that you are strong and you are capable. You have to find your own motivation, your own way to keep getting out of bed every day, even if you feel like shit. Remind yourself what you are doing it for and how you want your life to be. If you run straight to someone else hoping they'll make it better for you, it probably won't end well. And it's really not fair on them because

You have to find your own motivation, your own way to keep getting out of bed every day, even if you feel like shit.

you are choosing them not for who they are but for what you want them to do for you. It's a really tough one, but you have to find a way to be honest with yourself and recognize what you want and why you are doing the things you're doing.

Owning your shit

I'm so lucky H is here now. I think some people assume that our relationship is all fairy tales, cupcakes and rainbows, but it's really not. She went through hell with it – both when I was in the process of getting out of my previous relationship and afterwards, too. Because it's not like once I got together with H then everything was magically fine and we sailed off into the sunset. Of course there was fallout afterwards because I was dealing with a lot. And I still am. H was amazing and so loyal, even though it was a messy, difficult situation that was not of her making. She could have chosen a quiet life, but she didn't: she chose me, and the boys, who love her.

I think some people assume that our relationship is all fairy tales, cupcakes and rainbows, but it's really not.

It got even more complicated because after we split up, my ex went to prison for fraudulent trading. She'd gone to court once when we were still together and got a suspended sentence for

She could have chosen a quiet life, but she didn’t: she chose me.

something else, but then she was sent away for forty months. She was in prison for eighteen months in the end. It was a terrible time because my kids lost a parent and I had to say to them she was working away. Looking back, I made so many mistakes in how I handled that because I told the boys what she wanted me to say. (Though is there any good way to deal with a situation like that?) I took the kids to see her in prison and it was a horrible experience, but then she was moved to a different prison in London and I said I wouldn't take them that far. So none of us saw her for about a year.

Even when she first went to prison, after we had broken up, she still had a lot of influence over me, which was hard for H. My relationship history – including the toxic bits – had shaped me. You can't just shut yourself off from the person that moulds you. I thought, *who am I now? What am I supposed to be?*

I thought, *who am I now? What am I supposed to be?*

I think it probably helped that H and I were friends first and so she had seen what I went through. If I'd got together with someone brand-new a year after leaving my ex they might not have understood why I was the way I was. For example, I would bend over backwards to take the kids round to hers whenever she wanted to see them, even when it was late and I'd put them in their pyjamas. I didn't question whether I should have more of a say in the arrangements. When she came out of prison a year later, I wasn't the same person. I said, 'No, it's not all your way any more. You don't get to tell me when you're having the kids.'

H is sensible and kind. She's incredibly generous and never does something because she expects something in return. And it took me a while to get used to that. If you've never been in a controlling, toxic relationship it might sound weird when I say that it took me a while to adjust to being treated properly by someone who really cares about me, but if you've been in that situation, I expect you'll know what I mean. When H would take me on a date and be really good to me I didn't feel like I could trust it. My defences would go up and I'd say, 'Oh, you'll be gone in six months.' I just thought she would meet someone else or leave, or do something to hurt me. I couldn't believe she would stick around. I still say it now as a joke. I'll say, 'I give you six months,' and she'll say, 'Shut up, Charlotte, it's been four years.'

I had to learn how to be in an equal, loving relationship. At first, I couldn't accept that H was this nice person who was good with the kids, who didn't expect me to have her dinner on the table at five, didn't want me to lose weight. It was like a bit of my brain had been twisted around when I was in my previous relationship and couldn't believe H was for real, that she wasn't faking it. Sometimes I still act like a dick to her and I know it's because I'm testing the boundaries, on some level, to see if she'll react

I had to learn how to be in an equal, loving relationship.

the way my ex would have. But H never takes the bait. She'll just say, 'Have a day off, Charl,' and walk out of the room. She has so much respect for me that she'll just leave it be. And I have so much respect for her that I'll realize I shouldn't have done that. She's a saint.

'Have a day off, Charl.'

It's quite annoying, actually!

H proposed to me in Paris a few months ago. It was amazing, she did such a great job. I always thought I would know when she was going to propose, but I had no clue! Because it was around the time of my thirtieth birthday and H is a real romantic, I thought the trip was for that. We went on a dinner cruise along the Seine and then, when we got off, H said she wanted to go and see the lights of the Eiffel Tower that sparkle for five minutes every hour in the evening. I was a bit confused because we could sort of see them from where we were and H isn't normally into that kind of thing, but I went along with it.

The next light show was in ten minutes but we were an eleven-minute walk away so we thought we'd just jump in a tuk-tuk. But it ended up taking forty-five minutes – for an eleven-minute walk! It was a hilarious journey, though. We connected my phone to the guy's speaker and blasted out George Michael as he pedalled us God knows where around the streets of Paris. We got there eventually but had to wait for the next light show – and it was nearly midnight by then!

Then, just as they were starting, H got her phone out. I thought, *WHAT are you doing? You've made me wait ages for these lights and now you're looking at your PHONE?!* But she handed it to me and there was a video of the boys wearing t-shirts with 'Will you marry our Harry?' and shouting the same thing at the camera. It was so special, so unexpected, and obviously I bawled my eyes out.

Moving on

When a relationship ends badly, it's so easy to be angry with yourself, as well as the other person. Do you recognize any of these things that are so easy to say to yourself?

'I was so stupid for staying with them.'
'I was such a mug for believing what they told me.'
'I can't believe I trusted them, even though …'

That is so natural and probably just a stage you have to go through while you process what has happened and grieve the relationship. But at some point you do have to pick yourself up and say, 'That's done now. I can't change it.' You can't keep going back to it. Because so often we carry that through into our next relationship and go too far the other way, putting up barriers to protect ourselves like I did, and sometimes still do, with H. It takes courage to let someone else in when you've been hurt

It takes courage to let someone else in when you've been hurt before.

You deserve respect from everyone you let into your life but most of all from yourself.

before. But if you don't try then you risk hurting the other person because you are treating them as if they are the same as your ex, which isn't fair.

You're always going to have things in your past that hurt you and affect you. It's taken me a while to connect why I do certain things with stuff that happened to me in the past, but it's easier now I know why I'm like this. You have to face up to it, even the bits of you that you don't like or find hard to think about, if you want to get the life you want. You deserve respect from everyone you let into your life but most of all from yourself and that's hard if you're hiding from some truths. We all make mistakes, we all lash out and we can all push people away at times when they don't deserve it, but understanding why is the first step in forgiving yourself and moving on.

Now I'm in a good place I sometimes look back and think, *how could I have lived like that? Did that really happen?* It still pisses me off that I was in that relationship for so long. But I have to remind myself to let that go as much as I can. Because, as with everything, the truth is that if I didn't go through all

If I didn't go through all those things, I wouldn't be who I am today.

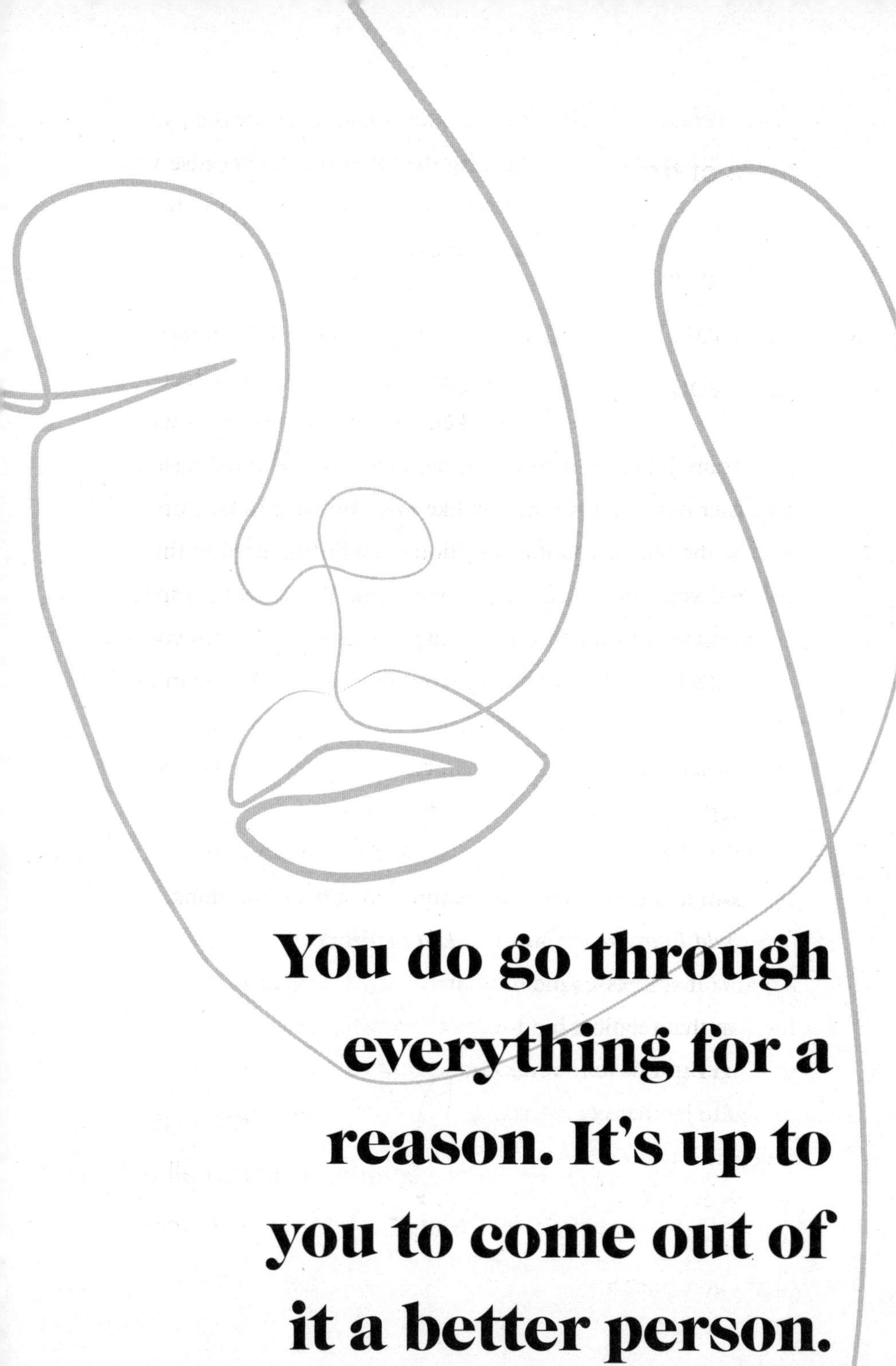

You do go through everything for a reason. It's up to you to come out of it a better person.

those things, I wouldn't be who I am today. Most importantly, I wouldn't have my beautiful boys. And at least I know how to cook, right?! You do go through everything for a reason. It's up to you to come out of it a better person.

♥ What love is ♥

Being with H has taught me so much about what it means to be in an equal, loving relationship. These are some of the things I have learned. Maybe you are happily single, which is bloody brilliant – don't let anyone tell you it's not. If you're with someone, I hope you are in a lovely relationship and you'll read this thinking, *duh! Obviously, Char!* But just in case you need to hear it, here goes …

- **I never feel the need to look at H's phone.** That was a big thing for me when I realized I had never even thought to wonder who she was messaging. Whenever my ex would go on her phone I'd almost swivel my eyeballs out of my head to get a look at her screen to see who it was. She would take her phone to the toilet and put it on airplane mode when she was out of the room.
- **I love doing things for H that make her happy.** But I don't feel I have to do things because I'm worried about what she'll do or say if I don't. There can sometimes be a

fine line between making an effort and wanting to please someone at the expense of what you want, but I understand where that line is now.

- **I dress how I want to dress.** H and I sometimes say, 'Me and you look like rats. We've been in four days straight, let's put on something nice and go out for food.' I never think, *H won't fancy me if I don't make an effort to put on make-up every day.*

- **I don't hide my emotions any more.** H never makes me feel like what I say is wrong. I can go to her with anything. Sometimes I might be talking rubbish it's true, but she'll listen to me and talk me through it.

- **Flirting with each other is fun and it's important.** I don't know how long we can get away with it until the kids cotton on and think 'eurgh', mind, but at the moment it goes over their heads! I still flirt with her the same as I did when we first got together. And laughing, too – making H laugh is one of my favourite things in life.

- **And so is date night.** You should always date your partner. It doesn't matter how long you've been together. Whether we go out or stay in the house, we make the time to enjoy each other's company. We do little surprises for each other, too. It doesn't have to be materialistic, and

Making H laugh is one of my favourite things in life.

actually it's better if it's not. It's about saying, 'I thought of you. I put the effort in.'

- **Little things make a difference.**

> H gets ready for bed before me and she always puts my toothpaste on my toothbrush for me and puts it on the side. She only ever forgets if she's drunk! It's a tiny thing, but it's ours and I love it.

- **It feels good to compliment each other.** You don't have to do it all the time or anything – but to be honest we do because we're cringy as fuck, haha! But I think it's important to say the stuff you appreciate about the other person out loud and not just think it and assume they know. Everyone needs the odd compliment when they're having a bad day. Little things like that from someone you love and who knows you really well mean so much.

- **You have to support each other.** I get more down than H does and she picks me up. And if she's having a down day, I'll pick her up. You've got to love someone that much you'll be their backbone when they need it and be ready to take the good with the bad.

- **We are strong because we're equal.** I don't ever feel I'm below H or she gets the final say. Whatever success one of us has is shared. It's not, 'You've done it' or 'I've done it'. Or, on the other hand, 'That's your job and nothing to do with me.'

Everyone needs the odd compliment when they're having a bad day.

- **You have to say sorry when you're wrong.** Partly because of some of the stuff I've been through and partly because I'm an attention-seeking knobhead(!) I do still act out sometimes. But I always admit when I've fucked up and say sorry (well, I whisper it. I still struggle a bit with that word!). I've had to learn that not every disagreement is potentially the end of the world and I know how important it is to H to apologize when I get it wrong.

- **Respect is everything.** I don't think I would have even really known what this meant before. H never belittles me, she always speaks well of me and she never talks down to me. It might sound mad that I didn't used to understand what this meant, but if you don't respect someone, how can you have a good relationship?

I hope this doesn't sound like I'm trying to say H and I have this perfect relationship where we agree about everything and never fall out. Of course we piss each

Respect is everything.

You've got to love someone that much you'll be their backbone.

other off sometimes – that's just life. But I'm so lucky that she has taught me how to trust someone, when I never had before.

Wherever you are now ...

If you're in a relationship with a wonderful person who you love, then I'm so happy for you. I now know how special that is. Hold them close, don't forget to compliment them, to listen to them and make time to go out and have a bloody good laugh with them.

If you're with someone who's great but you're worried they're not right for you, then take some time to try to understand how you feel. All relationships have their ups and downs and there are no fairy-tale endings. Talk to people who you can trust, but remember that everyone is influenced by their own personal experience so you can't expect anyone else to have all the answers for you – it always has to be your decision. Be completely honest with yourself, talk to the other person about how you feel and, ultimately, go with your gut.

All relationships have their ups and downs and there are no fairy-tale endings.

If you are in a relationship that's making you feel miserable and small, then know that you deserve so much more. No one has the right to take away your self-worth. Talk to people and get the support you need. It might feel impossible right now, but I promise you that you can start again and you will be so glad that you did.

No one has the right to take away your self-worth.

If you are single, then don't let anyone make you feel there is anything wrong with that. If you'd like to meet someone, then remember that sometimes the right person isn't who you might have expected, so keep an open mind. Don't settle for someone who isn't right because you feel like everyone expects you to meet someone, get married, have babies by a certain age. They can have their made-up timetable if they want, that's their business, but it's nothing to do with you.

Whatever your situation, the most important thing is to always care about yourself enough to know that you deserve love and respect from anyone you allow into your life.

Home Is Where the Heart Is

When Enzo, Brody and I moved into what would be the original Miss Greedy's Home on 3 August 2018, I thought this was going to be our forever home. After breaking up with my ex, it was the first house I had ever lived in that was just mine. I knew it was my chance to make a proper home for me and the boys where we could close the door and shut the world out. It was such a hard road to get there and I was determined to make it the very best I could. I wanted Enzo and Brody to grow up and flourish there. I wanted people to come round and admire it. I wanted to live somewhere I could be proud of.

The problems being of course that a) when we moved in the house was filthy and a bit of a shithole, and b) I had next to no money with which to pay for all these amazing ideas I had in my head …

I don't know where my love of interiors and upcycling comes from. At school, I liked art, but I don't think I was especially good at it. My sister's not really into it and my mum is terrible – she's got no eye at all! She'll put pink and some terrible shade of purple together and ask, 'Does this look OK?' But when I started watching videos on Facebook of how people had transformed ugly bits of furniture into something amazing, I was hooked. I just thought, *I can do that*. Even though I had about twenty quid to my name and some of the things I'd seen people do online looked expensive I thought, *there must be a budget way I can achieve something similar*. I knew I couldn't afford to buy new, but I could find the time to trawl Facebook Marketplace and eBay for some of the things we needed; I had the imagination to work out how I could transform them and surely a couple of cans of paint wouldn't cost that much …?

Making it real

My way of planning what I want to do to a room is to look for inspiration online and sort of collect ideas that I like – honestly, if I had a pound for every hour I've ever spent on Pinterest, I could

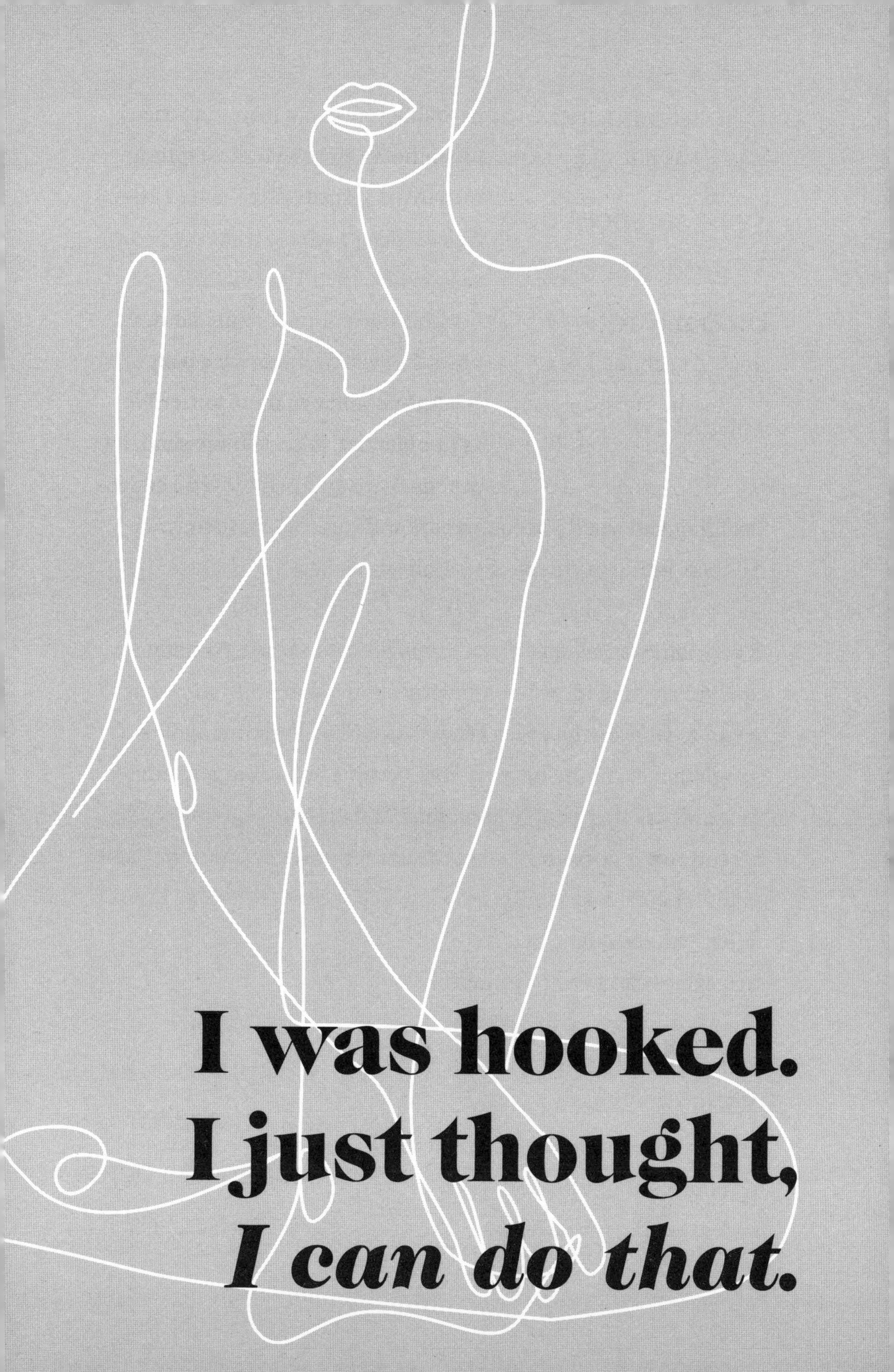

I was hooked.
I just thought,
I can do that.

If I had a pound for every hour I've ever spent on Pinterest, I could probably retire to a llama sanctuary tomorrow!

probably retire to a llama sanctuary tomorrow! I put them through my own 'Miss Greedy filter' until I have a clear idea of what I want the room to look like, then I just have to get it out and make it real! I can get quite obsessed, which might be a part of my borderline personality disorder. I'll say to Harriet, 'Can you imagine if we put this here and painted that in this colour?' And she'll just look at me and say, 'No, not really.' So then I just have to do it so I can show her.

There are basically two steps to the process for me. At the start it's about collecting ideas and thinking about what I like and what's going to work in the space I have. As well as Pinterest and just googling around the internet, my top tip is to look at Rightmove to see what other people have done in their houses. First of all, it's fun being nosy and looking at fancy houses online, but it's also really useful because you can see whole rooms and whole houses. What you see online and in magazines can be very beautiful but it's usually heavily styled and not really how people live. You might just see a picture of the corner of the kitchen, say, but on Rightmove you can look around a whole house

Look at Rightmove to see what other people have done in their houses.

and see where they've put their washing machine, for example, or what sort of storage they have. I look at the really expensive houses because often they will have used a decorator and it gives me ideas. It doesn't matter that you can't afford a bloody great mansion like that! You can still use these beautiful houses to think about what you are going to do in your own. If you're not sure about your own personal taste yet, this is a good way of getting a sense of what you do and don't like.

Then, once you've got all the inspo you need, step two is googling around to see how you can create the look at a fraction of the price. If you've seen an amazing farmhouse kitchen, put 'farmhouse table' or 'rustic furniture' into eBay or just google it and see what comes up. If you find you really like someone's panelled bedroom, google 'DIY panelling' and watch some videos. This is a good time to set your budget so you know what your price range is and to stop you getting carried away with, say, a sofa you can just about afford when actually you also need to buy paint and a rug and a TV table …

It's great to search through Insta and Pinterest and wherever else to figure out what you like, but on the other hand, it's important not to look at so many pictures that you forget to think about what will work for you in your home. You can find yourself thinking that the way a particular fireplace is styled looks amazing, but if you actually had that many candles you'd never stop dusting them, or you might even burn the house down.

Remember, it's your space and it's up to you what it looks like.

Realistically, you probably will be influenced by fashion. At least a bit. For example, I'm really into all the Scandi stuff that's been big for a while. And the latest trends affect what's available in the shops to buy, if you're getting things new. But even so, it doesn't matter what the current fashion is or what's in the magazines. Look at all the pictures you like of cool loft apartments with exposed bricks and those big metal lampshades, but if your style is more country cottage, then go for it. And you might love all the pictures of bright white living rooms with pale fluffy cushions – and then remember you have a toddler and a golden retriever. Fashions come and go, but this is *your* home and it has to feel right for you – and for the way you actually live.

When I have a clear idea of what I want to do I always make sure I know what I need to do it. How much paint? Does it need to be a special kind? What tools? What kind of masking tape? That sort of stuff. It's much more fun scouring the internet for beautiful handles for that chest of drawers you're upcycling than making sure you've got the right sort of paintbrush or primer, but I promise that life is much easier when you have the correct tools for the job. There are so many YouTube tutorials, Insta accounts and Facebook pages that can point you in the right direction here.

Fashions come
and go, but this
is your home
and it has to feel
right for you –
and for the way you
actually live.

Bargain hunt

If you see an expensive item you like, don't just give up and think, *well, I'm never going to be able to afford that.* Look for a cheaper alternative. For example, I wanted some really stand-out floor tiles in the bathroom, but they were so expensive and I would have had to pay someone to put them down for me so I went on the hunt for something similar but cheaper and found a roll of black and white stencil vinyl in B&M for £39.99 – which I was absolutely buzzing about. So, without a clue what I was doing, I bought some spray glue and fitted it myself, which was fiddly but still so much easier than I thought it would be. The effect was amazing! Putting the vinyl down transformed the room. (Though professional fitters wouldn't use spray glue all over – I'm not sure that's ever going to come off the floor!)

If you live in a rented place and you hate the bathroom or kitchen floor, then you may still be able to put some vinyl over what is already there, cutting it to fit and then either not gluing it or just putting a tiny bit in the corners or where it goes round a toilet or basin or something. That way, you will be able to roll it up and take it away if your landlord wants you to put it back to how it was when you moved in.

Similarly, if you see a piece of furniture you like, or any homeware items, but the price tag is a tad too expensive for your budget, search Facebook Marketplace, Gumtree and eBay for the exact same item. Try putting in the name of the model and also the brand and the item. Like 'Habitat rug', for example. You never know, it might just turn up.

Second-hand items are sometimes in immaculate condition, just not needed by the previous owner any more, so you can get a really good deal if you go on the hunt! I wanted a specific chest of drawers for Brody's clothes in our previous home. It cost £50 in the shop, but I found one on Facebook Marketplace for £10 – the effort of looking through eBay and Facebook was totally worth it because I saved £40.

You can get a really good deal
if you go on the hunt!

❀ Getting started ❀

If you're looking around where you live now and thinking, *yeah, I do actually want to do some work, but I've literally no idea where to start*, then don't feel you have to necessarily dive into a big, complicated project. If you don't yet have a clear idea of what you want to do, then start with some simple stuff and see how that feels. If you do some basic upcycling, then you'll pick up the skills you need for more complicated things that you can try next.

Things you can do right now to 'Miss Greedy' your home, for hardly any money …

- Find a quote or a motivational saying that's resonated with you. See if someone's created an artwork on the internet that also looks cool – or make your own – print it out, put it in a picture frame and hang it on your wall where you can see it when you wake up.
- Walk around your home and choose one thing that you've never liked – like a lamp, a coffee table or a bedside cabinet – and think about how you could change it or paint it. Go on Pinterest and get some ideas.
- You don't always have to go out and buy new things to make your space look better. Get your favourite jug out of a cupboard, or gather together some candles and some photos and make a display on a windowsill or sideboard.

Buy yourself a new mug so you have something pretty to drink your first cup of tea out of.

- Buy yourself a new mug so you have something pretty to drink your first cup of tea out of.

There are so many online tutorials and hacks that will help you make something amazing with next to nothing. Even if you think you won't be able to do something, then honestly, just give it a go. You'll be surprised at how easy some stuff is to do!

You really can paint ANYTHING

I have painted my kitchen sink, kitchen cabinets, front door and loads of furniture. There are a few simple rules to be aware of, but so long as you bear those in mind then you can paint pretty much anything you want:

- Do your research first and make sure you get the right paint for the job – not every paint works on every surface.
- Prepare properly. This is boring but you do need to make sure the surface you're going to paint is squeaky clean and not greasy or anything. You may need to sand it to give the paint a slightly rough surface to hold onto.
- Take your time and use masking tape if you have to – this will give you clean lines and stop the paint going on things you don't want it to.

- Clean up properly afterwards. Paint left on brushes and trays dries really quickly and is an absolute pain in the arse to clean! Bear in mind too that water-based paints are a lot easier to clean up than oil-based ones and don't smell as strong.
- Top tip: if you're halfway through a project and you have paint on the brush or in the tray that you'll need to use the next day, don't waste it by rinsing it out. Pop them both in a recycling bag and tie it tight. This will stop the paint drying out and keep the paintbrush moist. It will actually last for a while like that, if you've lost your mojo and you want to have a break and come back to it later.
- Always keep an eye out on Facebook Marketplace, eBay and particularly your local Freecycle or neighbourhood swap or gifting pages. Some people give away paint for FREE when they have finished a project and have a load left over!

Do your research first and make sure you get the right paint for the job – not every paint works on every surface.

I have two orange-tinted laminate wood wardrobes that I'm going to sand and paint soon. I'll also change the handles and panel the doors to make them look more expensive. Whenever I do a project like this, I'll set myself a budget and try my best to stay around that. It's always a good idea as it stops you getting so carried away that you spend so much money on fancy paint and handles that you probably could have just bought the thing you wanted rather than upcycling!

> Whenever I do a project like this, I'll set myself a budget.

When I transformed my front door in my old house on a budget, loads of people asked me how I did it. It was just a standard white PVC front door that I painted sage green and I bought a new door knocker for fifteen quid. I had to spend quite a lot of time cleaning the door and sanding it down first, and I put four thin coats of paint on it in the end (when the first one went on it looked terrible, but I carried on anyway!), but the work was totally worth it. The new tenants have kept it and when I drive past now and see it, it makes me so happy and proud. I hope they like it.

Shit happens

I haven't had any catastrophic fails (although now I've said that I've probably jinxed it and the next thing I do will go horribly wrong!), but there are a few things I wouldn't do again and there have definitely been some times when I've seriously wondered if something was going to work. There's usually a point in the middle of the process when it looks terrible and you can't see how it's all going to come together, but you just have to keep going and trust in the process. The first time I painted my kitchen cabinets I used a cheap paint because that was all I could afford and it took about three days to dry. That was stressful!

Keep going and trust in the process.

If something does go wrong or it doesn't work out the way it looked in your head, then pour yourself a glass of wine, take a deep breath and have a laugh about it. The main thing, if you are doing this for the first time, is to ask yourself, *can I afford for this to fail?* If it goes wrong, could you buy new paint or hire a sander or whatever would be needed to correct it? If you can't then it might feel like too big a risk. Something like a vase you can just chuck out is very

Pour yourself a glass of wine, take a deep breath and have a laugh about it.

different to something that's built into your house, like a floor. On the other hand, though, if you hate something so much that you can't stand looking at it, you probably don't have anything to lose. So go for it. Just make sure you do your research and you're not pushed for time and in a rush. If you don't put in the work to do the prep properly, then that's when things go wrong or paint ends up flaking or chipping.

You will learn as you go and discover your own hacks. I bought a mitre box which you can put a bit of wood in and it already has the angles, so you can make sure you cut it exactly right. I've also found that Gorilla Glue is perfect for lots of jobs – honestly, you could glue yourself to the ceiling with that stuff! But the point is, just have a go. Start something and see how you get on. Transforming something yourself and making it look beautiful and expensive for hardly any money is the best feeling.

The point is, just have a go. Start something and see how you get on.

My name is Charlotte and I am addicted to buying vases ...

Seriously, H has no idea how many vases I've secretly stashed away in the attic. I don't know what she'll say when she reads this and goes for a look! One of my

FAVOURITE things to do is to go on a charity shop hunt, mainly for vases or pots because I think they are SO useful. I have a few vases around my home that cost me 50p – yes, 50 bloody pence! Obviously, you can buy this stuff new, but pots and vases tend to be either expensive or a bit crap and flimsy if they are cheap. If you see a vase and you like the shape of it but it's not the right colour, buy it and spray-paint it – I love the stone-effect spray paint, which gives the vase a concrete look. You spray-paint the vase (or a plant pot) in a nice cream or white colour, leave it to dry, then use a stone-effect spray paint on top. The result is so beautiful and it costs a fraction of some I've seen online. It looks super-expensive, but it's so easy to do.

Have a sort out

If you have too much stuff or not enough places to put it, I promise that having a good sort out can have as much of an effect as if you'd just painted a whole room. I am absolutely mad for good storage as I think it makes such a difference when you can tidy things away easily. If you're a bit of a hoarder, go through your cupboards and gather anything you don't need any more and get rid. Or see if any of your friends want to do the same thing

I promise that having a good sort out can have as much of an effect as if you'd just painted a whole room.

and help each other out. You may even be able to swap some stuff – you might have what you consider the world's ugliest plant pot, but your mate could have a brilliant idea about how to upcycle it.

One of the first projects I did that I put on Instagram was to get a KALLAX cube storage unit from IKEA for Enzo's toys. I stuck wooden letters on the front of boxes that fit on the shelves with Gorilla Glue. It's something I've done a few times now and it's still one of my favourite hacks because it's really simple, you can easily put your own stamp on it and it works really well. If you've got kids you'll know what a mess they make with all their toys, so this was a way of teaching them to put things away and keep their things organized (not that it works all the time – it's not magic furniture!).

If you don't know what a KALLAX cube storage unit is, then look it up – they are so versatile and come in lots of different sizes. Often you also see them for sale second-hand. I made a sideboard out of one. I bought another eight-shelf unit and some plain white doors (which you can also get from IKEA – you can get loads of handy accessories from there), which I bought special stick-on wood decorative stencils for. And I got some screw-in legs from eBay (I've left it up on my Instagram, if you want to see the method). It was SO much fun to do and knowing I made it myself gives me such a happy feeling. It also meant I had somewhere to neatly store all those little things that just sit around cluttering up surfaces otherwise. (Well, I say that, but I mainly kept booze in mine and it was a bit heavy so it did end up

A simple thing like having an organized, restful environment where I feel I have control is really important to me.

bowing!) And then when I moved the room around I unscrewed the legs and turned it around so it sat vertically in an alcove. Just because you've already upcycled something once, there's nothing to stop you doing it again.

I've found so many times that depression and lack of motivation thrive on disorder and chaos. As someone who struggles with my mental health, a simple thing like having an organized, restful environment where I feel I have control is really important to me. So, what can you do to make your home better suited to who you are and the things you need to make you happy?

For example, if you like to cook, maybe you could focus on your kitchen (see the next couple of pages for my tips on how to revamp a kitchen on a budget). But it might also be a case of simpler things – like maybe you need a new (or upcycled!) spice rack so you don't need to pull out the whole cupboard when you're making a curry? Or have a look on Insta at my 'Greedy bin' that I hang over the cupboard door for scraps when I'm cooking. Honestly, it changed my life – and it went viral a while back – a bin did!

If you're constantly losing your keys, get yourself a nice bowl and sort out the hallway with a new shelf or small table for post, keys, umbrella, etc. If you fall over the kids' shoes every time you get to the bottom of the stairs, would a basket or a rack help keep things neat – and mean you're less likely to break your neck?! It's all about making your environment a happier and easier place to live in.

Upcycle your kitchen on a budget

Buying a whole new kitchen and getting it fitted is so expensive and just not an option for many of us. Or maybe you're saving up but you need to get a couple more years out of your current kitchen before you can afford a new one. It is absolutely possible to upcycle your kitchen on a strict budget, even if you're renting and you need to be able to reverse some of the changes you make. If you like cooking, you probably spend quite a bit of time in the kitchen so giving it a spruce-up makes a big difference. Here's what I learned from doing my 'Miss Greedy's Home Kitchen':

- New kitchen cabinets are really expensive, but if you paint the doors on the ones you have and change the handles (look on eBay – there are so many types available, but get ones that are the same size as your existing ones with the screws in the same place to make it much easier to swap them over), you'll feel like you have a brand-new kitchen.
- I even painted my worktops! The paint held up for years, though obviously kitchen worktops do get a lot of wear so it did need the odd touch-up from time to time, but overall, it was so worth it.

- Fablon is a brand of adhesive-backed plastic material that can be used to cover and decorate shelves, worktops, etc. Once you get the hang of sticking it down it gives you amazing results really quickly. (Just be aware that Fablon will melt if you put a hot pan on it so depending on how careful a cook you are, it might not be the right option for your worktops.)
- If you have a tiled area in your kitchen (or bathroom) that you hate but retiling isn't an option, you can get stick-on tiles to go over the top. I did this in my kitchen and they went on so easily and made the kitchen look completely different. They lasted well and peeled off lovely when I wanted to change them, so if you're renting and you despise your kitchen or bathroom tiles this is an easy solution that will make a big change.
- If you're not great at decorating I'd recommend going for a paint that has a primer in it (and with some projects you do ideally want to put down a coat of primer first anyway). A primer often means you won't need to sand down any surfaces before painting. However, if you want the paint to last longer, or if it's in a place that's going to get a lot of wear, sanding is always recommended.

You have the power to change things, even if it's only a few small things to begin with. It takes hard graft and determination to get a fresh start, but it's always going to be worth it.

Home is a feeling

I really hope you're sitting reading this somewhere warm and cosy that you love. I know not everyone is into interiors and DIY in the same way I am, but I do think that everyone needs and deserves a place of their own – whether it's council or privately rented or belongs to their family or they're lucky enough that they've bought it – where they feel safe and at home. If that's not you right now, then my heart goes out to you and I want you to know that things can get better. You have the power to change things, even if it's only a few small things to begin with. It takes hard graft and determination to get a fresh start, but it's always going to be worth it.

> I do think that everyone needs and deserves a place of their own.

When we moved into that first Miss Greedy's Home, we'd been living in a council house in a run-down area. You'd see lots of guys off their face hanging around and this one bloke would run around with a machete. There were always police in the street and I'd never let the kids go out to play. There were some lovely neighbours, but I still didn't feel safe. I managed to arrange a swap with a woman I found via a Facebook group, who needed to move closer to her kids' school, and the house she wanted to swap was in my dream location. It was where I'd grown up and near where I wanted my boys to go to school. I couldn't believe it.

In the weeks leading up to the day we were due to move I was on pins as I was sure she was going to pull out at the last minute.

She actually nearly did. On the day we had to do the swap, I got round there and she said, 'I can't do it, I'm not ready.' So H came round and we said, 'What if we helped move you?' And she was like, 'OK, thank you!' I think she just wanted someone else to do it all for her. To be fair, I think she had quite a lot of problems in her life. It was a bit annoying, but I really couldn't lose that opportunity so I just had to make my peace with it and get stuck in. Looking back, though, I don't know how we did it. We moved all of her stuff – her sofas, her fridge, everything – in H's little car. And moved all of our stuff in. Then we had to clean it. God, was it a mess. Fag ends and stuff everywhere – it looked like a drug den, but we did what we could with it.

The boys were with my ex that weekend and when they came back, they were excited to see our new place. I was so pleased they finally had a garden to play in – although the back garden was a state, we were fortunate enough to have a big front garden that just needed a mow. H and I had found some curtain poles in a skip and we made football goals out of them because I couldn't afford to buy some. Just watching the boys in their element

I knew then that we were home.

playing outdoors, kicking a ball about through this wonky goal with the mountains behind the estate in the background was magic. I knew then that we were home. That's one of my best memories from that time. Even if I could have bought them the most expensive toy in the world they wouldn't have been any happier – that's what it's all about, isn't it?

Turning points

I'm so glad I made it happen and got us into that place. That was such a turning point for me. From then on, everything was different. Don't get me wrong, it was still really hard. I had no money and I was still dealing with the end of the relationship I'd been in since I was sixteen. Plus, I was in loads of debt. I was not in a good place mentally, but at least now I was in a good place physically. I loved that little house so much (and it really was small – I could hoover the entire place without unplugging the hoover and plugging it back in again) and I loved what it represented to me.

In making that house a home for my boys I learned so much about upcycling and decorating, but I learned a lot about myself, too. I honestly believe that when you start to take control of the things that you can change, like your home environment, it can make all the difference. When you get used to making small changes, big changes start to seem more achievable.

When you get used to making small changes, big changes start to seem more achievable.

One really important thing I had to realize though is that for all I wanted my house to look beautiful, it is first and foremost a home for us. I was looking at all these beautiful houses on Instagram for inspiration and at one point I got it into my head that my house had, to look perfect all the time, too. Which is ridiculous. I've got two boys and now two dogs as well – it's not going to happen! I remember I got really obsessed with the cushions on the sofa and once the boys went to school I used to arrange them perfectly and then not sit on the sofa all day. Then when they got home I wouldn't let them on the sofa until I'd taken all the cushions off again. To be honest, it was probably to do with finally having a safe place that I was fully in control of – I think I got a bit obsessed. But that's no way to live, is it? You've got to be able to sit on your own sofa!

So, dream big and you will find ways to make where you live look beautiful, if that's what you want to do. But remember, it's your *home*. Walls get scuffed, kids put mucky handprints on stuff and sometimes the mess gets out of control. What you see on Insta are rooms that have been made to look pristine for a photo.

the most important thing is that it's your space and it should make you feel happy.

You ARE Worthy

Do you remember that bit in *Charlie and the Chocolate Factory* when Violet Beauregarde eats the chewing gum even when Willy Wonka tells her not to and she blows up into a giant blueberry and the Oompa-Loompas roll her away? Well, that was me when I had had Enzo. I didn't turn blue, obviously, but even after I'd given birth I was the biggest I had ever been and it really, really bothered me. I did some stupid things to my body because I thought I had to get back to looking how I did before I had a baby. When I think about it now, I feel a bit angry that I got my priorities wrong, but in the long run, I did learn a lot.

It feels like at every stage of our lives there's pressure on us to look a certain way and the temptation is to blame ourselves and blame our bodies for letting us down, for not being good enough.

Us women have always been judged more on how we look – since the beginning of time, most likely. I reckon there were probably women in the Stone Age worrying that their animal-skin tunic was making them look fat, feeling bad that they didn't look like the women they saw in cave paintings!

If you were a super-confident teenager who knew her body was still developing and was mostly happy in her own skin, then let me give you a round of applause and a piece of cake. Because that's how it should be. But for most of us, it doesn't work like that. Have you ever looked back on a photo of yourself when you were younger and thought, *I look great in that picture. Why was I so obsessed with how big my bum was/how small my boobs were/the spots on my chin?* I definitely have. And it's really sad because it gets in the way of us enjoying things and having fun.

Once puberty is out of the way and you have hopefully realized there are bits of you that you do actually like, then you might at some point decide to have a baby. And then your body changes all over again. You get stretch marks and nothing is quite so elastic as it was before. But you make your peace with that and then, as you get older, you have to deal with all the adverts for anti-ageing creams and society telling you that it's apparently not OK for women to get wrinkles or to be a bit saggy. To look older, basically. Which is mad because *of course* you're going to look different as you get older and what's wrong with that? Sure, there are all those celebrities who apparently haven't aged a day in the last twenty years – but it's not real! Isn't it a bit freaking weird

***Of course* you're going to look different as you get older and what's wrong with that?**

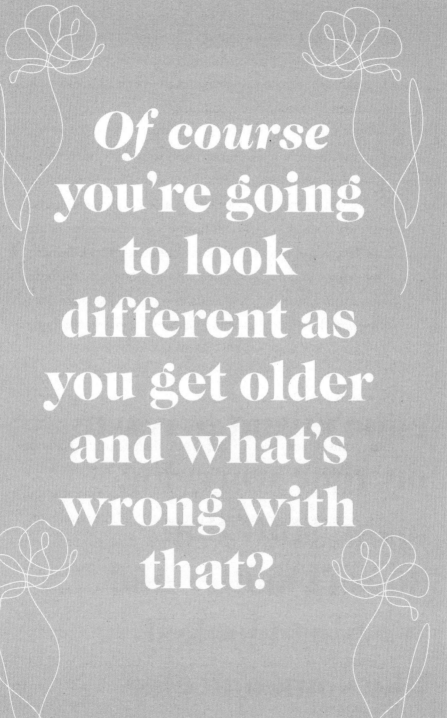

I don't want to waste my time worrying about stuff that doesn't matter and wishing I looked like someone else.

to think your body could go through all the stuff that happens in life and stay the exact same? I've felt insecure about my body at so many times in my life and I'm not going to pretend that I always feel great about it now. But I do know that I don't want to compare myself to other people any more. That I don't want to waste my time worrying about stuff that doesn't matter and wishing I looked like someone else. I'm not anyone else. My body has grown two beautiful boys, which is amazing. It is healthy and allows me to do stuff that I love, like play netball, go on walks with my dogs and dance round my bedroom like a lunatic – not everyone has that.

I can only be me and that is absolutely fine.

There's a lot on social media these days about 'learning to love yourself', which, don't get me wrong, is great if you can do it, but it can sometimes feel like another thing to fail at. It can make us feel bad about feeling bad! We are showered with airbrushed, filtered, Photoshopped women who have a team of make-up artists, stylists and professional photographers who are paid to make them look like that, so it's not our fault if we sometimes forget that it's not real. Women don't actually look like that! So we have to find our own ways of resisting being made to feel we have to look a certain way or we're not good enough, which is bullshit, while not beating ourselves up when and if we have days when we don't feel confident.

♥ The comparison trap ♥

I used to think that if I got down to a certain weight, I'd be happy. Then I'd get there and I didn't feel how I thought I would, I still wanted to lose some more. I'd look at someone online and think, *she looks about eight stone, if I get down to that I'll look like her.* Of course I bloody didn't.

First of all, we all have different bodies. Even if you do lose weight it's not going to make you look like someone else. We all have our own body shape and that's not going to change. Say you lose a bit of weight off your thighs, you might be pleased about that for a week but if you hate your stomach then you'll probably still hate it. I have never liked my big bum, but my best friend who's built differently to me always says, 'You're so lucky, I can never grow a bum. I've got an ironing-board arse.' And she's right – so you may as well learn to love your own bum. Harriet is built completely differently to me, she's naturally heavier than me, but I love her boobs, her bum and her legs. I could never get my body to look like H's because our bodies are different – everyone's body is. I can never fathom why H wouldn't like a certain thing on her body because I love it, but then she says exactly the same back to me.

You may as well learn to love your own bum.

Think about the women in your life who you love. Think about your friends. They're probably all built

We have to find our own ways of resisting being made to feel we have to look a certain way or we're not good enough, which is bullshit.

Your body is yours. It doesn't matter what anyone else looks like.

differently and some of the things they aren't that keen on about their own bodies are likely to be things that other people are jealous of. For example, someone thinks they're too tall, while everyone else is admiring their lovely long legs. Someone else worries about having a fat arse while their friends envy their hourglass figure. You might feel like a beanpole with no boobs, but your mates are all thinking, *I wish I looked that good in skinny jeans*. We are all different and that makes life interesting. Your body is yours. It doesn't matter what anyone else looks like. Famous or not, no one else's dress size has any effect on your life whatsoever.

The way I see it, we are always going to compare ourselves to each other. That's the way we're made. But realistically, no one is scrutinizing you the way you are yourself. No one is judging every little detail of your outfit the way you might have done in the mirror before you left the house. For one, they are all too busy worrying about their own stuff. If you think everyone has noticed and is thinking about how you've put on a tiny bit on your belly, I bet you a million pounds they're not! We all have a tendency to see ourselves as a collection of problems, which is really sad – 'My ankles are too fat/the pores in my nose are too big/my lips are too thin …' and on and on. But everyone else just sees …

No one is scrutinizing you the way you are yourself.

But everyone else just sees . . . you. And if they don't, it's going to be because they are unhappy about something in themselves.

you. And if they don't, it's going to be because they are unhappy about something in themselves.

You are never going to look like Kim Kardashian. And that's OK. Anyway, Kim Kardashian doesn't look like Kim Kardashian. She looks like a rich lady who spends a fortune on doing all sorts of things to her body, whose business relies on her always looking like a completely unrealistic version of what women actually look like. She can't pop down to Tesco for a pack of biscuits in her oldest pair of joggers because the media would go insane and she's got a whole brand resting on how she looks. It must be knackering. I for one am very glad I am not Kim.

I promise you that none of these things are 'problems':

- Cellulite – aka, skin that isn't totally smooth. BIG FUCKING DEAL!
- Scars – tell the story of things you survived.
- Belly rolls – fine, we all have them.
- Mum tum – your body grew a human being. That's AMAZING!
- Wobbly bits – unless you're made from wood, bits of you will wobble.
- Birthmark – a mark that is totally unique to you is not only fine, it's actually pretty lush.

- Stretch marks – bodies change over time. That's normal. That's LIFE!
- Acne – I just googled it and most of us get it at some point. It is normal and fine.
- 'Bingo wings' – give them a flap for me!
- Literally anything else – also totally fine AND TOTALLY NORMAL.

Mum tums and baby blues

When I was younger, I was an absolute twig! I don't want to be that skinny again. With borderline personality disorder, you can be very all-or-nothing about things. I used to be obsessed with dieting. It wasn't just about being thin: because of how my life was then it was also about control. I was unhappy a lot of the time and I didn't feel like I was in control of a lot of what was going on, in my life, but my body and how much food I put into it was one area I felt I could control, so I got obsessed with that. It wasn't good and it wasn't healthy.

And then I got pregnant with Enzo and became a human blueberry. After he was born, I thought my body would just go back to how it was before because no one told me what to

Unless you're made from wood, bits of you will wobble.

expect. I actually think it's quite fucked up that you have all those appointments with doctors and midwives but no one tells you what it will be like after you've given birth, that your body will change and you will still have a 'bump' for a while.

I had a difficult birth with Enzo and then I got home and my body was a mess. I was only twenty-one and I didn't know that happened. I'd been used to being this skinny little thing, but I'd had the baby and I still looked like I was pregnant. I thought there must be something wrong with me and I felt embarrassed about it. There's definitely not enough support for people who have body dysmorphia or struggles with their body while they're pregnant. You can see why people get depressed. You've got a new baby who's crying and all the stress of new parenthood and you feel like your body is an absolute car crash.

So, I went on this mad diet. It was probably an eating disorder, thinking back now. I won't tell you what I ate, because if you're someone who does or has ever struggled with disordered eating, then you don't need to hear about that, but it was next to nothing and all while figuring out how to be a mum for the first time. It makes me so sad now that my first thing after having a child was that I needed to look how I used to look. My body had made a beautiful baby, but I was obsessed with looking the same as before I was a mum. Of course my body had changed, *I* had changed. But I couldn't see that.

These days, more celebrities are honest about their post-baby bodies, but when I had Enzo, the media was obsessed with how famous women 'got their figures back' after giving birth and loads of people were bringing out post-pregnancy diet and exercise books. I hate that – it makes so many new mums feel shit and all so they can sell you a book or a DVD (or both). The reason these celebrities got back into their old clothes so quick was because they had a personal trainer telling them exactly what to do. And they probably made themselves bloody miserable while they were doing it. Take it from me, the last thing you should be doing after just having a baby is stressing about how quickly you can start wearing your old jeans again. Maternity clothes are comfortable, wear them for as long as you want. I had a favourite pair of maternity jeans from Mothercare with this stretchy black band at the top. I wish I still had them now. The band that went over your stomach was so comfortable and smoothed you out – it was like a bra for your tummy rolls. Why did I ever get rid of those? So, figure out how best to look after your baby and yourself and I promise you everything else can wait.

The last thing you should be doing after just having a baby is stressing about how quickly you can start wearing your old jeans again.

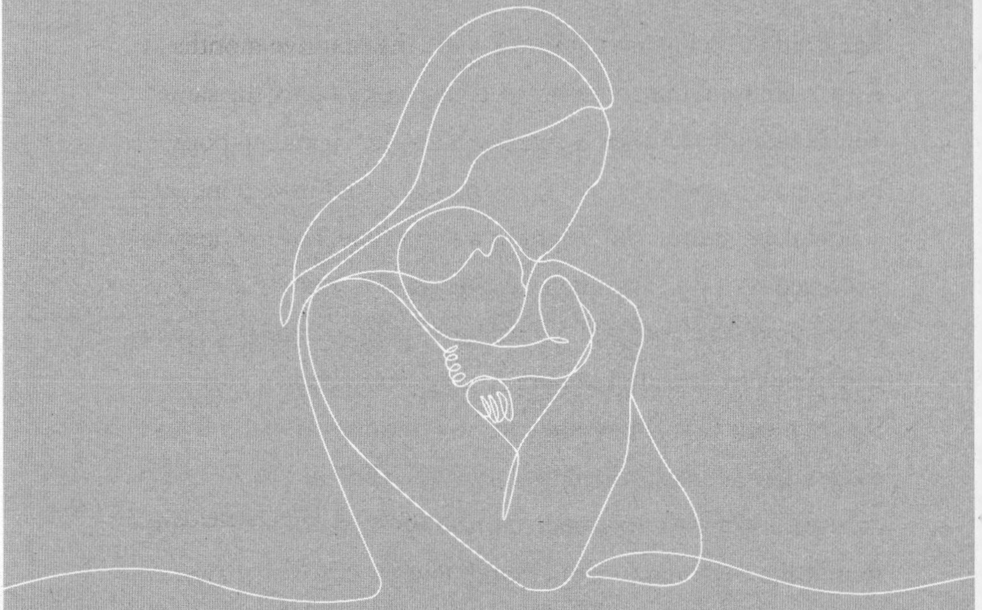

Figure out how best to look after your baby and yourself and I promise you everything else can wait.

But I didn't know that then, so I spent the first five months of Enzo's life thinking about how I could look exactly the same as before I had him. I didn't give my body the chance to bounce back on its own terms, as I know now it would have done. I lost a ridiculous amount of weight in a short time, but my body had stretched so it was like I had this saggy prune on my belly and little raisin boobs with nipples facing to the floor. I wore Spanx pretty much every day for years, even when I was thin again, because I thought everyone would notice my saggy mum tum through my clothes and it was shameful and unacceptable.

I didn't give my body the chance to bounce back on its own terms.

A lot of my friends had babies around the same time and I thought they looked amazing and I was embarrassed because I thought I looked terrible. Of course, I never saw them naked. I'm sure they had stretch marks and saggy bits, too, but I didn't think about that. For all I know, they had their own insecurities and they were looking at me and thinking I'd done well to lose the baby weight (which I absolutely hadn't).

When Enzo was nine months old, I decided to get a boob job. I thought that my girlfriend was looking at other women and she wouldn't fancy me any more with my deflated boobs. Now, I'm not judging anyone else here. If you've had work done or you're thinking about it, then it's your body and your choice. It's none of my business. But I did it for the worst, most unhealthy reasons.

And I really regretted it. I don't have that really elastic skin that some people are blessed with and seven years after I'd had my implants put in, they'd moved around and dropped down. They became really painful, especially the left one, and I had to have a mammogram to make sure it wasn't something serious. I'd come to really hate them so I had them taken out. After that, I felt less lethargic so I do think they caused me problems health-wise. I would say that if you are thinking about having something like this done to make you feel good, do think about how it might look in ten years' time and how it might affect your health. It's important to properly think it through and get lots of expert advice. Could you afford to have your implants taken out if you change your mind or they don't look how you thought they would? If I hadn't had the money to get them taken out when I did, I would have been stuck with pain in my chest, feeling lethargic and implants somewhere down near my belly button.

When I was pregnant with Brody, I carried the emotional scars of what had happened after Enzo's birth and I really didn't want to put on weight like I did before. I enjoyed being pregnant with Enzo more because I thought I could just gain two stone and it would magically melt away. But then with Brody, I was so scared of getting big again that I didn't eat enough even though I was pregnant, and then I went back to the gym within six weeks of giving birth. I was bad to my body, which was really stupid and I wish I hadn't done that.

If you're pregnant or you think you might want a baby in the future, then please know that your body will change but that's a

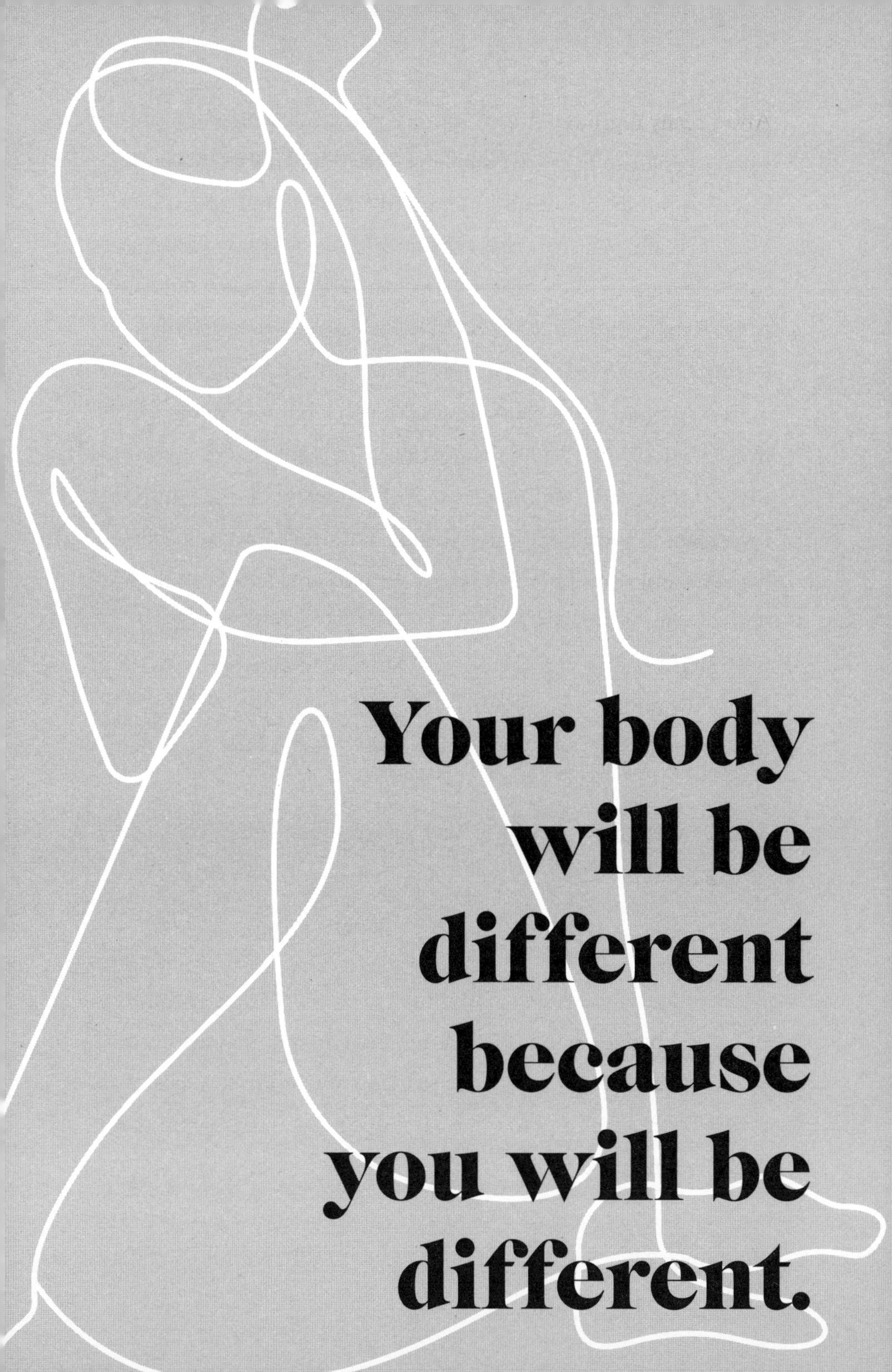

Your body will be different because you will be different.

Remember that you deserve to be happy.

good thing. It will be different because you will be different. If you can, please try to see your stretch marks and scars as a reminder of the amazing thing that your body has done. Anyone who tries to tell you that mum tums are bad, that you have 'let yourself go' is talking ABSOLUTE SHIT. And if you're struggling, particularly if you have had issues with eating disorders or disordered eating in the past, please reach out and get the help you need – whether that's from friends and family or professional help. Tell your GP if you think you need to see someone and don't shut up until you get what you need. Whether you're a mum or not, remember that you deserve to be happy.

The baby bubble

I'll stop talking about babies and birth in a minute, but I just want to say one more thing that I wish I'd known when I had my boys, in case it helps someone else. A baby is a newborn for such a short period of time and you really have to try to make the most of it.

It can be a scary period, it's true, while you get used to being a parent, and it's not the easiest time for everyone, but what I've learned from getting it completely wrong is how important it is to enjoy the 'baby bubble' – those first few weeks – as much as you are able in your own situation and not to let anything get in the way of that. Not how you look, not anyone else's expectations – nothing at all. It's about you, your partner and your new baby. Here are some of the things I've learned ...

- People will offer to bring you food. Say YES! They won't keep offering forever. DON'T, like I did, turn down all offers of dinner because you think you have to be the perfect mum and do everything yourself. Now I would love to sit on the sofa while people brought lasagnes to my house. What was I thinking?!
- Lots of people will want to come round to see the baby. Say NO! At least until you are ready. DON'T, like I did, allow a constant stream of anyone you've ever met to come to the house whenever they want. It's not about them, it's about you. And let's face it, all babies look pretty much the same when they are that tiny – at least, to anyone who isn't a parent or grandparent. Your mum's friend and your auntie's next-door neighbour can wait.
- When you do allow people to come over, you might feel you have to make yourself look good like the celebrities in the 'new baby' photo shoots for the magazines. DON'T, like I did, put on your holding-in pants and straighten your hair because you think you have to or people will judge you. I promise it

The baby bubble is all about enjoying your little unit. It's this really short period where the real world can fuck off for a bit, and I learned the hard way that it's important to make the most of it.

doesn't matter what you look like at this point and don't let anyone make you feel like it does.

The baby bubble is all about enjoying your little unit and not worrying about anything else you'd normally do. It's this really short period where the real world can fuck off for a bit, and I learned the hard way that it's important to make the most of it.

Be the woman you needed when you were a girl

A while back, I put a picture of my mum tum on Instagram with a shout-out to all the women who were still working on accepting their bodies, whatever that means for them. I had so many messages about that post from women who had also felt ashamed of their bodies at times. A few were new mums who got in touch to ask how I learned to love my post-baby belly as they were struggling to accept theirs. Which made me feel really sad as I can remember

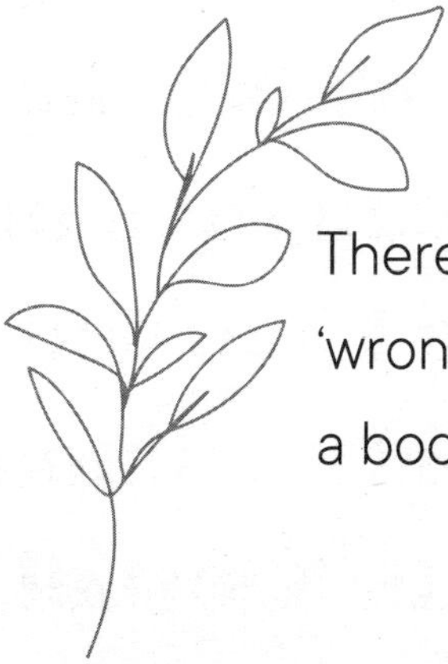

There's no 'wrong' way for a body to look.

We're drowning in pictures of what we are told to believe are 'perfect' bodies, but who decided that, anyway? Who made the rules to say this is how you have to look to be acceptable?

so clearly how I used to feel. There's no easy answer other than you'll do that over time, by being kind to yourself and reminding yourself that there's no 'wrong' way for a body to look.

We're drowning in pictures of what we are told to believe are 'perfect' bodies, but who decided that, anyway? Who made the rules to say this is how you have to look to be acceptable? And if you're this size or this shape, well, sucks to be you because you don't pass our test! I didn't make that rule and I definitely don't remember signing anything to say that I agreed with it.

I think that things are changing and we're starting to see a wider range of bodies in the mainstream media and hopefully the next generation will feel less pressure to be a certain size or shape. But in the meantime, I think there are some things we can all do towards accepting and maybe even loving our bodies. And that is to be open and honest and, most importantly, to accept each other.

I believe that real women cheer each other on.

I think the strongest women are the ones who are open about the times when they don't feel very strong. We all have a responsibility to stand up to these stupid beauty standards that aren't even real and remind each other all of the time that we

ARE worthy. Think about what you needed to hear when you were a teenager or those times when you've felt the most insecure and alone. Imagine you had the best big sister in the world who said exactly those things and would never dream of judging you. Now be her! Or if you can't be her all the time, at least be her as much as you can in the way you talk to yourself and the way you talk to others. Because there are girls and young women coming up behind us who need to see women being honest about their bodies – the good and the bad. We all need to see that.

We ARE worthy.

❀ Your body is ❀ AMAZING!

Seriously, stop and think about it right now – what does your body do for you? Does it let you play with the kids in the garden? Go dancing? Either in a club or round the kitchen when you're getting the tea. Does it let you go swimming in the sea or running in the park? Does it keep going even when you've been rushing around all day and you've not had the time to feed it properly? Maybe you've run a marathon, maybe you've given birth, maybe you've survived a serious illness. But even if you haven't, remember our bodies are amazing and carry us through our daily lives without so much as a thank-you.

Get a pen right now and make a list of things you'd like to say thank you to your body for. Try to get up to five things if you can. Here's a spot for you to do it …

The Five Things I'd Like to Say Thank You to My Body for Are …

1.

2.

3.

4.

5.

We need to stop punishing our bodies for not being the size or shape society tells us is 'right'. Remember those rules are completely made-up rubbish and start being kinder. This is what being kind to my body means to me. What does it look or feel like for you?

- Accepting that I'm not failing if I don't always love every part of my body every single day.
- Reminding myself that if I don't, that's massively down to how many images of 'idealized' bodies are forced on us every single day. It's not my fault if I internalize some of that, it's only my fault if I accept it without question.
- Not starving my body – it needs fuel to function properly.
- Not bingeing on rubbish – my body deserves proper nourishment in return for everything it does for me.
- Reminding myself that exercise feels good, I just have to be bothered to go and do it.

I'm not failing if I don't always love every part of my body every single day.

Don't get me wrong, I don't always do a good job of all of this. My main problem is that I think I must have a snacking disorder. I can eat fifteen bags of crisps in a half-hour. It can get to the point where my insides are screaming at me to eat a vegetable and I constantly have a bad tummy. That's when I know I have to really sort myself out. It's not good, but as soon as I have just one week of being healthy I feel better in so many ways.

And by being healthy, I don't mean following the latest fad diet or making all my vegetables into weird spirals and pretending it's pasta. I mean eating three proper meals a day in sensibly-sized portions and trying not to eat too much sugar or rubbish foods I know are no good for me. It means fruit and veg and making sure I have enough nights off the booze.

Sorry, wine, you know I love you,
but sometimes we need to take
a break from each other!

I love food, I love cooking and I love going out to eat with H and having a date night, just the two of us. I love taking the boys out for a treat and teaching them about eating out and how to behave in a restaurant (that sometimes works better than others!). Nothing beats a hot chocolate with marshmallows AND cream AND fudge pieces and I'm definitely not ever giving up the Terry's Chocolate Oranges. I do have to remind myself to eat healthily when my snacking disorder gets the better of me, but I can do that and not feel like I'm depriving myself of the treats I love, too.

What are your go-to healthy foods?

I don't think dieting really works in the long term. You might get rid of a few pounds and that's fine if you want to do that, but I think working on having a good relationship with food is the best plan, although I do absolutely understand that's easier for some of us than others.

One small thing you can do is to think about what foods you genuinely enjoy that are good for you AND nourish that amazing, remarkable body of yours. If you decide to go on a health kick and you're sitting there with a bowl of crap iceberg lettuce and no dressing, then that's a bloody miserable lunch and of course you're going to be tempted to reach for the Guylian chocolate seashells.

If you need to, make a list of all the good things you like and stick it to the fridge or take a picture on your phone so you can look at it in the supermarket. We've been trained to think 'naughty' food is automatically a treat because it's forbidden, and that can make us obsess about it or at least want it more. It's all just food at the end of the day, and we need to work out how to step away from that kind of unhelpful thinking.

If you show up to a class and everyone is really snooty and judgemental, then you have my permission to bin it off. Remember, real women support women.

Exercise is meant to make you feel good, not bad

God, the complicated relationship we can get ourselves into with exercise! And it really doesn't help seeing all those celebrities on Instagram where they're bending over in a pair of ninety-quid yoga pants or smugly showing off a six-pack. I'm still working on finding the best exercise for me, but I know that trying to make myself do something I don't enjoy is never going to end well and will most likely just mean I give up and feel even more shit about myself.

I'm still working on finding the best exercise for me.

I really love playing netball. I train once a week and play once a week, but I'd probably play every day if I could (goal attack, since you asked). It works for me because it's competitive and I like being part of a team. And it's on set nights of the week so I don't have to decide when to do it and motivate myself to make it happen – it's all arranged and I know when I'm going (plus my girlfriend is the coach so I don't have loads of choice!). So based on that, the best advice I can give is to figure out what might work for you, if you don't already know. Do you like having some time by yourself and listening to loud music? Are you more likely to show up to a fun, energizing class? Do you like feeling strong and lifting weights?

It's OK to try something new and decide it's not for you, though don't beat yourself up if you're not good at it to start with. It can take a bit of time. You wouldn't tell your kids to give up immediately if they had a go at a new sport and they weren't instantly good at it, would you? No. (Or at least I hope not!) So, give yourself a chance. If you feel like other people are judging you, then they're probably not – they are likely so focused on not falling flat on their faces while doing the yoga move that they won't notice anything you do. (Though if you show up to a class and everyone is really snooty and judgemental, then you have my permission to bin it off. Remember, real women support women.)

If you want to try something new but you're feeling unconfident, don't forget that there are videos on YouTube for everything under the sun now. So, you can always have a little practise at Pilates/Zumba/karate/whatever in the privacy of your own home first so you know what to expect before you show up to your first class.

Ditch the things that make you feel shit

The diet and fitness industries are big business and so are the cosmetics industry and the fashion industry. There's nothing wrong with that in itself, but it does mean that a lot of people are trying to make money from selling us stuff based on making us feel we have to look a certain way. We have images of these 'perfect' bodies shoved in our faces all the time and unless you never look at social media, magazines or a TV ever again, there's not a lot you can do about that. But you do have control over some of the things you let into your life, so if something is making you feel shit, then try to figure out why that is and whether you can eliminate that negativity from your life. For example:

- Unfollow accounts on social media that only show perfect, idealized bodies. Replace them with accounts that inspire you.
- If you have a friend who is constantly talking about dieting or criticizing other women for the way they look, politely ask them not to. Be kind, because they might be doing it because they feel bad about themselves. But if you feel that they are having a toxic effect on your life consider whether they really deserve a place in it.

- Don't squeeze yourself into clothes that are too tight for you. Our bodies change throughout our lives – that's normal. I kept my size eight jeans for ages because in my head if I could still somehow squeeze my body into them that meant I was a size eight. But that doesn't work! We all deserve to be comfortable. If you are wearing clothes that don't fit, then you will subconsciously feel like you are too big. That's not the right way around – the jeans are too small.
- Don't keep clothes that don't fit you any more. You're setting yourself up for failure and depression every day when you open your wardrobe to get dressed and half the things in there don't work for you. Go and find some other things that fit your body now and make you feel good.

We are all beautiful

It's hard to love your body all the time. In fact, unless you're very lucky, it's probably impossible. It's difficult to resist the pressure we are constantly under the whole time as women and all the messages we get telling us we are only worthy of love, praise, success, care if we look a certain way. But that is BULLSHIT and I think deep down, even when we're feeling low, we always know that at some level so we need to remind ourselves and each other of the following as much as possible:

You are beautiful.

You are strong.

You are enough.

You are capable.

You are worthy.

You ARE NOT Broken

Being mentally well is the best thing ever. When I have a good day, I'm like a jack-in-the-box. I feel really energized and I get loads done. It's easy to do all the right things – I'll get up and have a good breakfast and go for a run. Then I'll clean the house while dancing around to music. I'll sit down and get my work done without putting it off for ages and I'll be really productive. I'll think, *this is the best feeling in the world. I'm going to do this every day. This is what my life is going to be.* Then of course the next day something changes and I can't do anything. It feels so frustrating because I know exactly what made me feel good the day before, but either I can't motivate myself to do it or I just don't enjoy it as much. So why does your mind decide that today is a day you're going to be sad and force you into a depression you don't want to be in? It feels so unfair.

I have always struggled with my mental health and in the last few years I have been diagnosed with borderline personality disorder (BPD). One of the symptoms is being quite all-or-nothing. So, while I have days when I have so much energy and feel really positive, the flip side is that there are other days when I can't even get out of bed. I won't do my work, go on Instagram, leave the house. If I'm not in a good place, I can spiral quite quickly and go from being fine to really low. Just a few things going wrong, or just feeling wrong to me, sets it all off. I used to be in denial and force myself to go on my Instagram stories and look really chirpy and happy. I didn't really talk to anyone about how I felt because I thought if I could ignore it, then it would go away. But that made it worse. And it's not honest. I've now learned some techniques to make myself feel better, but I've also learned that it's OK to just have that day when you lie in bed and eat all the carbs and ride it out. I'll at least try to do some work and get some housework done, but sometimes I just need to take a step back, to spend a day on the sofa watching shit TV, knowing that tomorrow I'll get back into it.

It's really important to be kind to yourself in that situation.

It's still a work in progress, definitely, but I feel like I learn more about what can work for me and my mental health every few weeks. I try to strike the balance between not completely giving in

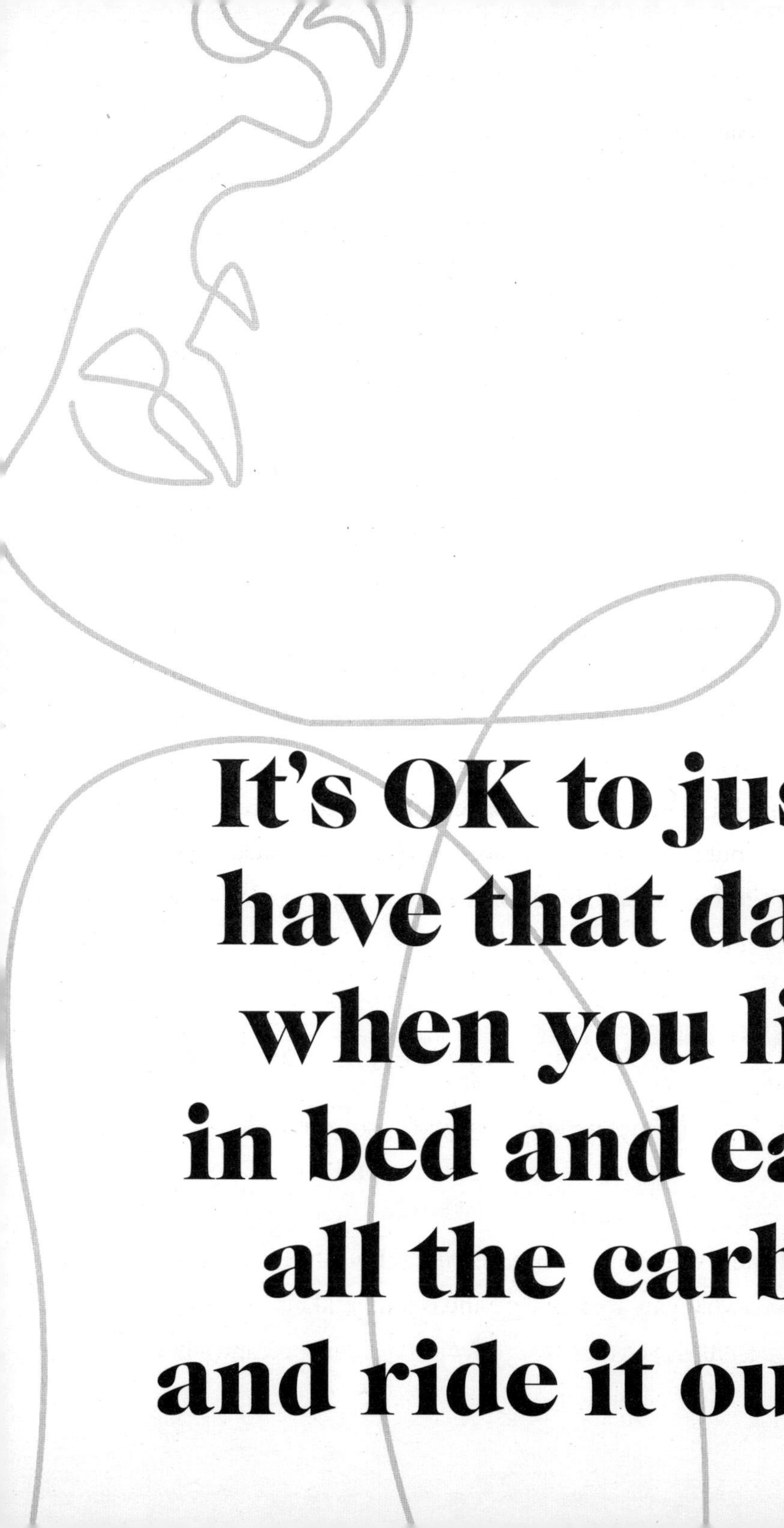

It's OK to just have that day when you lie in bed and eat all the carbs and ride it out.

and wallowing but also recognizing what I need, and if that's just to take some time, then that's what I do. Below are some of the things that I find help me keep my mental health in balance. What about you? When you've been through a bad patch and you're starting to feel better it's good to consciously think what helped you so you know what to try next time.

Cold showers

After I get up, I have a five-minute cold shower. If you've never done it before then it might sound like the worst way to start your day, but I swear it will change your life. You'll probably only be able to do it for about fifteen seconds to start with, but you'll soon build up to longer times. Honestly, when you get out, you feel like you're just running on endorphins. I keep seeing all this stuff online about how it's apparently really trendy now to go on some sort of retreat and do cold water therapy. But just turn on the cold tap! It's that bloody simple (and a lot cheaper, too!).

Making my bed

Mentally, I don't think I can start my day until I've made my bed. There's a quote I really love: 'If you want to change the world, start off by making your bed.' And I know I'm going to have a bad day if I don't do it. I love making my bedroom feel like it could be in a hotel. I straighten all the covers and make everything look really neat and tidy. Then I plump up the cushions, put them carefully back on the bed and roll back the top of the duvet like a flat sausage. It might seem pointless to some people, but it gives me a really good feeling when I've done it. It's a really important part of my morning routine – I do genuinely feel I can change the world when I've done it!

Music

When I get up in the morning, I have to put music on. I have an uplifting playlist and it really helps me to face the day. If I don't put music on, I slump around and I can't get going. If you're even a bit into music, I really think curating some playlists of stuff that makes you feel good is worth doing. It can be one big playlist you add to whenever you think of or hear a song you like or you can make different ones for different times – like exercising, cleaning, first thing in the morning. The only rule is it has to be songs that make YOU feel good, not that you think you should be into because other people say that band is cool, or that your boyfriend or girlfriend likes to listen to. It only works if the playlist is yours. If the cringiest and cheesiest song in the world makes you feel good, then stick it on there!

Oh, and sing along.
As loud as you can without the neighbours banging on the walls!

Fur babies

I know not everyone can have pets and they are a huge responsibility. Plus, they can make an absolute mess. I spend so much time cleaning up mud and fur from around the house – honestly, at one point I realized I had washed both the dogs but forgotten to bath my son Brody! But for me, spending time with Kobe and Minnie works wonders.

If you don't have any fur babies in your life, then you can still go and spend time with someone else's. Lots of people would appreciate a bit of help with dog walking/cat sitting/hamster minding. There are websites like borrowmydoggy.com that connect dog owners with people who'd like to take them for walks and charities like the Cinnamon Trust (cinnamon.org.uk), where you can volunteer to help someone look after their animal while they are in hospital or unwell.

Eating good things

This one is NOT always easy for me! If you feel a bit shit then the temptation is to reach for the crisps or the chocolate because at least then you get that little hit of sugar in your bloodstream and it makes you feel better for a second. Or you feel like you are giving yourself a treat. And I think that's completely fine. Do what you need to do.

BUT if you're doing this a lot, then it might not be helping you in the long run. I know I feel better when I eat properly and get enough fruit and veg in my diet. Realistically, your body and mind aren't two completely separate things, are they? So, if your guts are a mess because you've only been eating junk, then it's not going to help your brain feel better. I can only speak from my own experience, but I know that I have to strike a balance with this.

Being honest about booze

If you follow me on Instagram, then you'll know how much I like a glass of wine. (If you don't, the answer is: a lot!) Whether it's sitting on the sofa at the end of the day watching telly, or going out with Harriet for food, I enjoy having a glass of rosé in my hand! But I have to be honest and recognize when it's not doing me any favours and I need to give it a rest for a bit. Drink is a depressant and it does affect my mental health, making me feel more anxious or grouchy the next day if I overdo it. I call it alcohol anxiety. Even if I've only had a couple of glasses the night before it can still happen. I've had periods when I've realized I've had a drink every night and thought, *Char, you're taking the piss out of your own body and mind here*. And I've stopped. I'm lucky that although I have an addictive personality in other ways I have never had a problem just stopping for a bit.

If you drink, then I think the most important thing is to realize when it's making you feel crap and do something about it. You might need to keep a diary of what you've had to drink and then how you felt the next day, or give it a miss for a couple of weeks at least to see how that makes you feel. There's loads of info online about this and if you need another motivation, check out Sober October, which is a challenge to give up booze to raise money to help people suffering from cancer.

The most important thing is to realize when it's making you feel crap and do something about it.

If you think you might have a problem with drinking or any other addictions, then please care enough about yourself to reach out and get some help. You only get one life and you deserve for it to be AMAZING!

So don't suffer in silence and don't let shame stop you.

Create and connect

When I split up with my ex, I stopped seeing a lot of our mutual friends. I still had my very small group of best friends, who are amazing and were so supportive, but when I started @missgreedyshome on Instagram it showed me how good it is to have some sort of network of like-minded people and it doesn't matter if that's online. Getting inspiration from other people's accounts, getting messages from people who followed me and knowing that people liked my ideas made a huge difference at one of the hardest times of my adult life. Back then, I didn't have

It takes effort to break out of that cycle, but you *can* do it.

many followers and so I could reply to everyone who messaged me, which I loved doing. All those people who I chatted with via message or who left nice comments on my posts couldn't have known what they were doing for me, but it really meant the world.

Having a creative outlet of some kind is so good for your mental health and if you can find a way to share that with others, then that's even better. Feeling isolated or lonely is the absolute worst if you struggle with your mental health, but it can be a vicious circle because if you're down and you're a bit lonely, it's going to feel harder to try something new and connect with people, so you're more likely just to stay in and feel worse in the long run. It takes effort to break out of that cycle, but you *can* do it.

Having a creative outlet of some kind is so good for your mental health.

I started my Insta account because I loved upcycling and learning how to do DIY projects on a budget. I play netball because I'm competitive and I love being part of a team who want to play their best and win the game. Whatever it is you like to do, there will be a tribe out there who are into the same thing and will cheer you

Don't forget what it's like to be the newbie and look out for people who seem a bit lost and need welcoming into your gang.

Whatever it is you like to do, there will be a tribe out there who are into the same thing and will cheer you on. If you can find them, they will lift you up and make you feel good.

on. If you can find them, they will lift you up and make you feel good. If you already have them, then don't forget what it's like to be the newbie and look out for people who seem a bit lost and need welcoming into your gang.

January blues

All these things I've just been talking about are the things that I have learned keep me mentally healthy. But they don't always work and I accept that at some times things will be harder than at others and that's OK. It doesn't mean I'm failing or that my life is going wrong. For example, last January, I was going through a hard time and I got myself into a whole month of not being able to do much, when every day I found myself struggling to get out of bed, not achieving very much and then beating myself up for it. I kept saying that tomorrow I would get back on top of things, but I couldn't seem to do it. I tried all the usual things, hoping the next day I would just wake up and everything would be fine, but it didn't happen and I didn't know how to get out of the hole I was in.

It got to about 20 or 21 January and I said to myself, *right, I'm going to stop promising myself that tomorrow it will all be different, because I've been saying this since the beginning of January and it's not worked*. Instead, I decided I was going to focus on the following Tuesday, which was 1 February. For the next ten days

I accept that at some times things will be harder than at others and that's OK. It doesn't mean I'm failing or that my life is going wrong.

it was still hell and I wasn't doing the stuff I should be doing and I felt like shit, but I knew I was getting closer to the day I'd promised myself I was going to get on top of it, so I focused on the little things and tried to get myself a bit better every day.

I made myself stop drinking and eat a bit more healthily. I didn't go on some mad health kick, eating only spinach and quinoa or anything like that because I knew it wouldn't have worked; I just left the sugar alone as much as I could and made a conscious effort to eat some more fruit and veg. Even when I really didn't want to, I got up, I had a cold shower, I put my music on and I got dressed. Rather than getting obsessed with all the work that was piling up that I couldn't face, I focused on the stuff I thought I *could* do. Even if it was only small things like cleaning the oven or sending some overdue emails, at least they gave me the sense that I had done *something*. (Actually, I think often we should be prouder of the small win we fight for on a bad day than the big shiny achievement we make when everything is going well.) I managed to get my head away from the all-or-nothing thinking that can come with BPD and slowly weaned myself off the sofa and into a better headspace. OK, I know that might not work for everyone, but it worked for me. It was the first whole month I'd had of being really down and it was horrible, but at least it taught me what to do if I find myself back there again.

Your lowest point is not who you are.

If you ever have times when you feel really low like this, then I'm so sorry because I know how shit it is. All I can say is that you

Often we should be prouder of the small win we fight for on a bad day than the big shiny achievement we make when everything is going well.

have to forgive yourself and remind yourself as much as you need to that although poor mental health may unfortunately be a part of your life sometimes, it doesn't define you: your lowest point is not who you are.

If you are close to someone who goes through these periods, please be kind and please be patient. No one would choose to live like this. If you have never been in this situation personally, then you might find it harder to understand why someone can't just get it together, get in the shower and carry on with their day. Unfortunately, that's often not how it works – our brains can feel like our worst enemies sometimes.

If someone you love is suffering from poor mental health

If you've never struggled with your own mental health it's totally understandable if you don't know how to help someone in your life who is going through a tough time. The truth is that everyone's different and there is no magic wand. You can't fix someone, or cure them, and it's not like if you cheer them up enough they'll snap out of it – it obviously doesn't work like that. You can support them, though, and make things feel a little bit more manageable. You can't make them get up and have a shower, but you can turn the shower on for them, find them a nice fluffy towel and bring them a cup of tea after. H does SO MUCH for me and she is amazing at knowing what I need when I am having a bad day. Here are some of the things that I have found really helpful:

- **Listen:** H always listens to what I have to say, even when it might sound like I'm being over the top and a bit dramatic. She lets me say whatever I want and doesn't make me feel like that's wrong. Sometimes getting out all the thoughts swirling around your head and telling them to someone who you know won't judge you makes a big difference.
- **Stay calm:** I don't know how I managed to end up with such a bloody saint but somehow H never loses it with me. She doesn't get annoyed or impatient with me and her staying calm makes me feel calmer.
- **Be kind:** H doesn't boss me around or assume that she knows best when I'm having a bad mental health day, she just does things that make it easier for me to do what I need to do to start feeling better. It helps that she knows me so well. For example, because she knows making the bed is so important to me, sometimes she'll do it when she can see that I'm not going to. You can't force someone to do something, even if you are convinced it will help them – you just have to be there.

Me and BPD

I know that when lots of people who are struggling with something – physical or mental – finally get a diagnosis that gives them a word for what's wrong with them it can be reassuring or even a load off their mind. Like, 'THAT'S why this thing feels so much harder for me than it seems to be for everyone else.' But partly because of what was going on in my life at the time I was diagnosed, and also probably because of previous encounters with doctors as a kid, that wasn't my experience. Four or five years ago, being told I had borderline personality disorder made me feel like shit, but now I'm in a much more stable place and I understand more about what it means, it's good to be able to put a name to what's going on in my brain.

It's good to be able to put a name to what's going on in my brain.

I went to the doctor because I was always angry and I knew I needed to sort my shit out. I was still with my ex so there were obviously lots of reasons for this. But when I was told I had BPD, I left the doctor's office and cried. When they said there was something wrong with me but they couldn't give me anything for it, I just thought, *what am I meant to do now?* The doctor said I could go to therapy and support groups, but I didn't want to at that point.

Borderline personality disorder is also sometimes called emotionally unstable personality disorder, though a lot of people don't like these terms and find the labels unhelpful. It's related to how you think and feel about yourself and your relationships. There's a whole list of things that can indicate you have BPD and if you experience enough of them, then you might be given that diagnosis. These include feeling things very intensely and having strong emotions that can change quickly, so you might find you go from feeling great to really shit in just a few hours. You can feel empty and/or act impulsively and some people with BPD self-harm or have issues with addictions.

The best way I can describe how it is for me is that it's like my brain can go at a hundred miles an hour. I have big highs and big lows and there's almost nothing in between. I can flip out and feel really shit over tiny things. Sometimes I say horrible things to H, which is really unfair, but she is so, so patient with me. Forming stable relationships is something people with BPD often struggle with because we can push people away to test their commitment. Fear of abandonment is something else that can come with BPD and that's definitely something I have. It's why I say to H, 'You're probably going to leave me anyway.' To which she just rolls her eyes! Control is also a big thing with me. It used to be around my relationship with food and then it was cleaning and tidying the house. At the moment, though, I feel that's much less of a

It's like my brain can go at a hundred miles an hour.

problem and I don't feel as obsessive as I used to. Or, at least, I get obsessed in a way that doesn't have a negative impact on my life – like making my bed! (Karate chopping cushions is also very good therapy.) So, things can change.

It really is exhausting sometimes and can send you spiralling into a hole that you then don't know how to climb out of. Lots of people with BPD get depression or self-harm. I self-harmed quite badly when I was younger and depression has been an issue for me. When I was told I had BPD, I didn't want to know. But since then I've learned a bit more about it and that really helps. I don't know which parts of me are because of it and what's just my personality and I can never really know. But it doesn't really matter in a way because it's all me, at the end of the day, and I have to accept that's who I am and manage the bad stuff as best I can.

I've also realized there are some positives, too. We BPD people have some special traits! I think it makes me really headstrong and determined, which can be a good thing. People with BPD are often very creative, too. On my best days, I am the happiest person in the world and H says that it's great to be around me.

At the end of the day, I have to accept that's who I am and manage the bad stuff as best I can.

That's the trade-off for the terrible lows. I'm also really loyal and when I do let someone in, I'm incredibly protective of them. I have a chart on my phone that lists all the good stuff that BPD can bring for you, which I look at sometimes when I'm experiencing more of the bad things.

Borderline personality disorder affects every part of my life. As soon as I wake up, my brain is buzzing. One side of my brain is telling me all this negative stuff and the other side is being positive and saying, 'No, today is going to be great.' H calls my negative side Patty. Every time something really negative comes out of my mouth, she will say, 'Oh God, it's Patty again.' We've turned it into a joke and sometimes laughing about it is enough to shut down the negative thoughts. (But it works because it's our shared thing – it's never like H is taking the piss out of me.)

I don't have any easy answers for anyone who has this or any similar mental health condition, as the fact is it can be really shit at times and how you deal with that is always going to be quite personal to you. But I do think we need to talk about it more as people need to know that they are not alone and there is absolutely no shame in it.

> Sometimes laughing about it is enough to shut down the negative thoughts.

Feel better

Anyone who tells you that someone with mental health issues just needs to 'cheer up' or 'get out more' is obviously ignorant and a complete bellend. In my experience, though, there are ways I can manage my mental health and make myself feel better when I'm not at my best. They don't work every single time because there is no such thing as a magic solution, but this is my advice:

- Put some good music on and move your body – that's always a good start. Try making your own playlists (*see also* page 149).
- Get out of the house and go for a walk, especially if it's sunny.
- Aim to always make your bed.
- Hug your dog. Or stop a friendly dog in the street and hug that.
- Buy yourself a bunch of flowers, a fancy coffee, a new nail varnish. Something small that says, 'I deserve a treat and I deserve to feel better.'
- Do some cleaning or decluttering. That might sound boring if you're not a cleaning fan like me, but if you can't sort your head out today, it might make you feel a tiny bit better if you can at least sort out the mess in just one of your kitchen cupboards.

- Talk to someone. It doesn't have to be an epic chat about all the things that are going wrong, just a funny WhatsApp chat with a mate about nothing in particular can be enough to get out of your head for a bit.
- Run yourself a bath. Tell everyone in your house you need ten minutes' freakin' peace and lie there in the bubbles and breathe. Focus on the good things and, as much as you can, try to let the bad things drift away.
- And finally, don't blame yourself if none of this works. Sometimes it won't and you just have to ride it out and try again tomorrow.

My tattoos

When Enzo was little he used to ask me about the scars I have on my arms, left from when I self-harmed as a teenager. I didn't know what to say so I told him that our cat did them. (But he then went around telling everyone the cat had attacked me and no one wanted to go near our old cat. Which just goes to show that there are no easy answers when you're a parent!) When they are old enough, I want to be able to tell Enzo and Brody that when Mummy was younger, she was so sad and couldn't tell anyone and the only way she felt like she could get the sadness out was by hurting herself. I will tell them that they never have to feel like that because they can talk to me about anything and they never have to bottle anything up like I did. But right now, they are too young for that conversation, so it was our naughty cat who made the marks on my arms and a shark who did the ones on my legs.

The scars on my left arm were the most noticeable and I got the sleeve tattoo to cover them in 2014, mainly so Enzo couldn't see them. Then in August 2020 I decided to get the tiger on my right forearm to cover the scars there. I had done an ad for washing machine tablets where the scars were quite visible and I got a lot of messages about them. It's natural that people would ask questions and a lot of them sent messages because they had also self-harmed in their past, but I just wasn't able to talk about it then. This was back when I still thought that I had to hide the 'bad' parts of me that society found 'unacceptable'.

I don't regret my decision to have my tattoos – because there's no point regretting anything that makes you, you, and also because I have some beautiful artwork on my arms. That said, if I was back there, knowing what I know now, I wouldn't choose to cover the scars on my arms again. I haven't covered the ones on my leg – I wear what I want

There's no point regretting anything that makes you, you.

We shouldn't be ashamed of anything, least of all the times in our lives where we struggled but got through all the same.

now and I don't try to hide them. I'm not bothered any more if people see them when I'm wearing shorts and I don't mind them being visible in photos like I used to (I used to edit them out). We shouldn't be ashamed of anything, least of all the times in our lives when we struggled but got through all the same. I used to be ashamed of my scars, but I understand now that they are part of who I am and they don't make me weak or unacceptable.

♥ Don't hide your scars ♥

I don't want anyone to think they have to be ashamed of any part of themselves. I love to celebrate strong women, but that doesn't mean that I think we have to be strong every single day. Always remember …

You are not failing if you have a bad day.

- You are not failing if you have a bad day.
- You are not a loser if you feel too sad to get out of bed.
- You are not broken and you are not weak. Mental illness may be part of your life, but it does not define who you are.
- Mental health struggles are real and they are bastards, but believe in yourself, get the help you need and things will get better. There are organizations offering free help and advice, so reach out.

Mental illness may be part of your life, but it does not define who you are.

Rock bottom

There have been two points in my life that, when I look back on them now, really make me wonder how I'm still here. Twice, I have been in the most horrendous place mentally and I tried to take my own life. I don't think anyone around me ever knew how low I was. I was always good, and still am good at times, at hiding how I really am. I recognize that it is sometimes a scary, powerful and dangerous thing to be able to do.

When I was sixteen years old, I couldn't understand why people around me were constantly abusing my trust and my love. I was still reeling from what had happened with the person in my life who had taken advantage of my vulnerability. Then, one night, my girlfriend at the time wasn't answering my messages. She'd turned her phone off, and it was enough to tip me over the edge. I went out drinking with one of my best friends, and on the way home, I just totally broke down. I threw myself in front of a bus and if my friend hadn't pulled me off the road I would have been flattened within seconds. I'll never, ever forget that moment, sitting on the ground being cradled by one of my best friends, my heart breaking because I just didn't want to live any more. I can still see it so clearly in my head and I am devastated for that girl who thought life wasn't worth living any more. If my friend hadn't been there, I wouldn't be here today. The next day I made out like I fell and pretended I was fine. I was scared the girl I loved would leave me if she knew, so I acted like everything was normal, ignoring all the warning signs that showed I was literally at rock bottom.

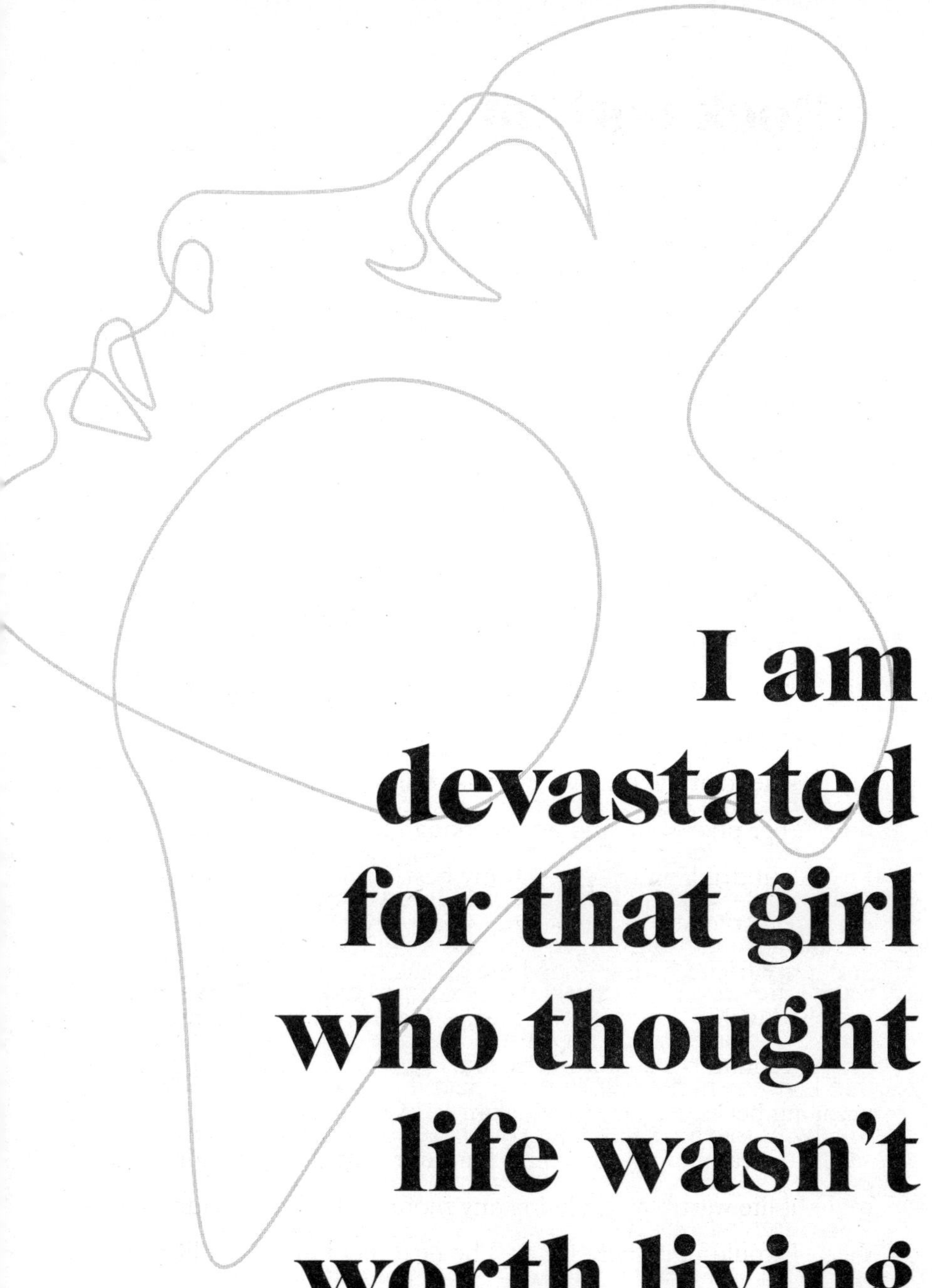

I am devastated for that girl who thought life wasn't worth living any more.

Then, another time, while still pretending to be happy Greedy, I was at a house party and I took a load of pills I found, expecting and praying to just fall asleep peacefully and not wake up. Though all that happened was that I was violently sick and then severely hungover. My friend asked why I'd taken the pills and I pretended I'd just wanted to take some drugs. She still to this day doesn't know that, in truth, I just wanted to disappear.

I am so grateful to be here, full of scars from arms to legs, beautifully imperfect with my tiger stripes.

You're probably wondering why I'm telling you about these incredibly dark and painful times. The point is that I am SO GLAD that those two attempts to take my own life failed. I felt like I had no one, like the world would be better off without me and the people who I loved I didn't deserve because they treated me like absolute shit. I'm so glad that I survived to learn that it wasn't the case. Back then, I was just a bad judge of character and kept loving and caring for the wrong people. I know now that I am worth more than those people and they were never worthy of me. So, I'm telling you these stories in case you are ever in a position like I was where you feel alone and worthless – because you are NOT, my babe. You are an incredible human and this world needs you. You are so loved and so deserving of a wonderful life. Even if it's hard to see that right now from the bottom of the hole you have found yourself standing in, I promise that it is true. I am living proof that life can change and you can be happy. Sometimes it just takes longer to get there, and you just have to keep holding on.

My cousin Dewi took his own life on 23 December 2021 and everyone around him, including me, was heartbroken. I understand that he was in a lot of pain and I wish he knew how many people loved him, how many people there were around him who would have helped him and who thought the absolute world of him. I couldn't save my cousin and it hits me in the pit of my stomach every day.

I have learned to talk a little more than I used to. It's still a work in progress, but it is so important. And I have found ways to deal with my emotions when I am going through a rough patch and my mind is trying to tell me that I'm not worthy of this life. For me, my therapy is the beach, the sea air, the waves, or soft music by my favourite artists and looking at photos of my children. Yours may be something else – try to write down a few things that make you calm and your soul feel happy. You'll find these can become little coping mechanisms that will help you through so much. I go to the beach whenever my soul hurts and it brings me back. It's my happy place and the ocean has definitely saved me from myself more times than I can write down. Where is your

I have learned to talk a little more than I used to. It's still a work in progress, but it is so important.

happy place? Is there somewhere you feel grounded and that heals you?

There are a couple of things I've discovered that I keep coming back to. The first is to just stop and put your hand on your heart when you're feeling overwhelmed. Feel your heartbeat and know that you have purpose. You are here for a reason and it's so important to remember that. Another is this quote: 'Friends and family can't rescue you if they don't know you need it. So ask for help to fight for another day.'

Where is your happy place? Is there somewhere you feel grounded and that heals you?

It's so important to spread the word that there's nothing 'wrong' with you if you are experiencing mental health problems. We need to talk about them. Yes, as I know only too well, there are still horrible people out there who say if you talk about issues you have experienced, you're just doing it for attention. It is a fucked up world we live in in some ways, but I still believe that if you are struggling, you should be able to speak about that without judgement. If you ever come across somebody who tells you 'just get on with it', or that you're attention-seeking, then you have to cut that person out of your life because it's going to make you go even further into the pit. Let's all be honest about our low points so we make it easier for others to reach out when they feel vulnerable and alone. Let's tear down any shame around poor mental health and, more than anything, let's look after each other.

Do It, Be Bold

I get lots of messages from people asking me how I got started on Instagram and more generally how I have the confidence to do what I do. The question about confidence is not an easy one to answer, not least because we are all different and good at different things. But it's true that I feel so different now to how I did when I put up that very first post, or the first time I dared to post a video of myself (though, I do have wine to partly thank for that!). So much has changed for me over the last few years and I feel so much more confident than I did back then. I want to try to figure out where this confidence comes from and how you can get the courage to jump in and not let other people's opinions – real or imaginary – hold you back.

Let other people lift you up

I've spent a lot of time in this book talking about making your own rules and figuring out what you want from life, rather than what other people expect from you, and I completely stand by that. But that doesn't mean we don't need other people in our lives to lift us up. I've already told you about how much Harriet's support means to me (sorry if that made you feel a bit sick – we do wind each other up sometimes!) and how my best friend Emma helped me to get out of a toxic relationship. But the people – complete strangers, mostly – who have sent me messages on Instagram, who have liked and commented on my posts, have made such a difference to my life, too.

Back when I first moved into the original Miss Greedy's Home I was such a mess. I was in the very early stages of making a new life for me, Enzo and Brody, and, to be honest, I don't know now how I got through every day. It was H who reminded me I'd set up that Instagram account, though I hadn't done much with it yet, and she said I should post about the new house. At first it was just an outlet and a way to record what I was up to as I did some DIY and started turning what was a bit of a dump into a home for me and the boys. So, it was kind of a shock when the number of people following me kept going up

To be told one little good thing, even just that I'd made someone smile, was gold to me.

and up. And when people started saying nice things about what I was posting, I was made up.

When I turned the camera around on myself and got even more positive reactions it felt amazing. All through my life, I'd been told I was hard work, or I was mental, or that I'd never make anything of myself. To be told one little good thing, even just that I'd made someone smile, was gold to me. To have something that was my own and for people to say they were enjoying my stories and my posts was such a new experience and it did really help with my confidence.

I loved it so much (and still do) when someone got in touch to say that they'd used an idea from one of my upcycling projects and made something themselves. I still can't get over it when I do something in my house and it inspires someone else to give it a go, too. Then, when I started sharing a bit more about myself, like about my mental health or showing my mum tum, and people began messaging me to say that they were struggling with some of the same things and my post had helped them or given them a boost … wow! Honestly, that healed me. I don't care if that sounds over the top – it really did.

That's the very best of social media, isn't it? That connection with people you have never met that makes a difference to your day.

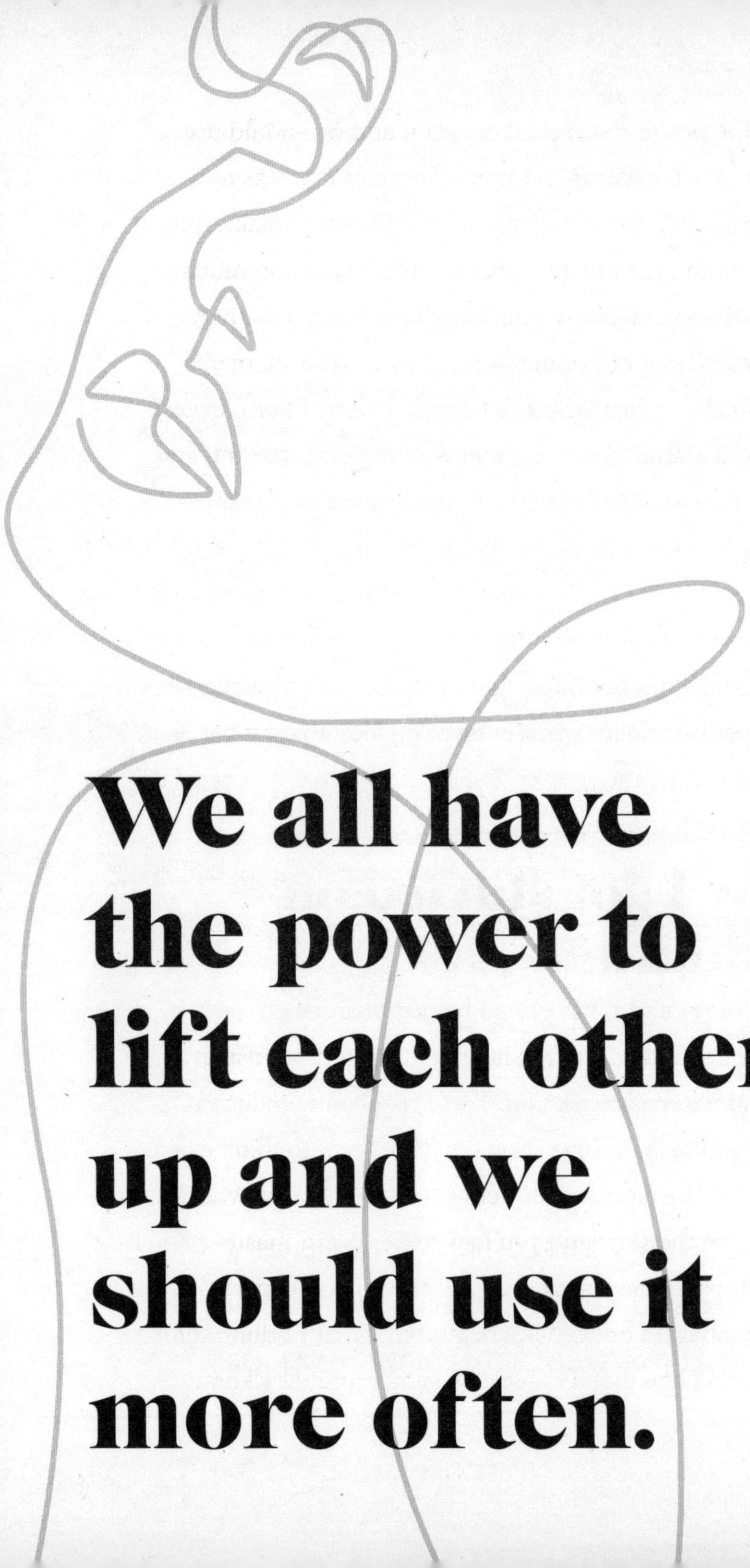

We all have the power to lift each other up and we should use it more often.

We all have the power to lift each other up and we should use it more often. I will never forget how important that was to me at that really tough time in my life, so I always try to make sure I remember to do the same for other people. There's so much negativity in the world, but we can all put out some positivity and push the bad shit out of the way. It's true on social media and in real life, too. Whether that's complimenting your partner, reminding your friend how great they are when they've had a bad day or even just telling a random person that you like their outfit.

Confidence does come from inside, it's true. You can't live and die by the approval you get from other people, but we all need good people around us to remind us of all the things about us that are great, particularly on days when everything feels that bit harder.

How I got started on Instagram

When people get in touch to ask how I got started on Instagram, I think they sometimes mean how did I get so many followers or how did I start making money. Some people seem to think when you have a lot of Instagram followers you cleverly knew what you were doing from the start and you had some sort of master plan. I mean, that probably has happened with some people, particularly if they have managers or agencies behind them, but I don't think it generally works like that. People engage because they know you're being yourself, because they are into some of the same stuff as you and they like watching people who are like them.

Back when I had just moved into Miss Greedy's Home and had barely twenty quid to my name, I just wanted to make my house look good on a budget. That's all I cared about and it was amazing to be able to find a community of people who liked doing that too. I found it really helped with my mental health because, when it comes down to it, upcycling is all about changing something you really don't like into something you do. With imagination, a bit of work and maybe some Gorilla Glue. A bit like life, really! (Though Gorilla Glue doesn't work in every area of life, unfortunately – I have tried!) The sense of achievement I get from that is one of the things that makes me feel more confident and I think that's what people were responding to on Insta when they first started following me: I was just being myself and doing something I really cared about.

Upcycling is all about changing something you really don't like into something you do.

I didn't realize you could make money off Instagram. These new rules came in and I started to see some accounts sometimes put up posts that started with {Ad} but I didn't know why. Then one day an eco-cloth company called E-Cloth contacted me and said they'd send me some free cloths. I was over the moon because they were my favourite cloths and they were something like £4 a pop at Tesco. They said, 'When you post about it, make sure you put "ad" because it's gifted.' And I thought, *Ah, that's what that means. It's gifted.* A bit later, someone I used to talk to a lot on Insta asked what I charged for ads. I didn't know what she meant and I said I'd had some cloths. She explained that companies were willing to pay you if you talked about their products because – whether you meant to or not – you're doing advertising for them.

Not long after this, I fell in love with Gousto, the food subscription box. It's quite expensive but I had a code where someone could try it and get 60 per cent off and I would get a £15 credit for more food boxes. It was great because lots of people were using it to try out the service, which meant me and the kids could eat really good food for free, which was amazing for us. But then Gousto messaged me and explained that there was this platform called Awin that they used and I could go on that. Anyone who used my code would still get the same deal but it would be better for me. Once it was up and running, I checked it to see how it worked and it said that I'd made £250. I couldn't believe it! It got all the way up to £4,000. I rang H and told her that we were rich. I was always living in my overdraft then and had never seen that much money before. I mean, I'd barely seen £200 all at once

I was always living in my overdraft then and had never seen that much money before.

in my life! That was the point when I realized that my Instagram could be work, as well as a hobby I'd come to absolutely love.

I'm telling you about this partly because it's quite a taboo subject and I think people should be honest about how it works. It's quite a new thing to be able to turn your passion into a business in this specific way. Lots of people don't get it and can be really dismissive of social media, which is fine, of course. It's not like you have to use it. The older generation often don't get it (my dad definitely doesn't understand what I do!) because many of them don't use social media so much. Advertising is all around us all the time, after all, and people want to know what products are out there. If you've used a face cream for years and you want to tell your followers why you like it, and the company will make money off that and wants to pay you to do it, then I don't think many people would turn that down.

Now I want to be really open about how this all works – I don't think people on Insta are always honest enough about it. I only ever work with companies I love and products I really do use. (I got asked to advertise a sex toy once. I was like, 'Er, WHAT?! No.') I'm in a really lucky position and I'm picky about who I work with. I turn down a lot of work because I know it's not who I am. I do understand how people can get carried away and want to say yes to every company that approaches them, which means their whole Instagram

I turn down a lot of work because I know it's not who I am.

Find something you are good at, that you love – if you haven't already – and keep doing it.

becomes work. I won't ever do that because I always want it to be my hobby and my safe space. So, although it is a job for me, and one that is great because it lets me be at home with my children and pick them up from school, I don't get carried away and forget that the most important thing is that it's something I love doing. I would never put money over being true to myself or the way I really live. I'd rather never make any more cash from Insta but keep my followers, as that's what means the most to me.

There are some people on Instagram who are tactically trying to set up their account as a business from the get-go, or who have their heads turned by companies offering them money, and that's fine for them – you do you – but it can mean that people start thinking that's what every influencer is doing, which is a shame. I didn't start using Instagram because I wanted to start a business. Sharing the things I was making for my house and talking to other people about DIY and upcycling became such a passion for me and everything else followed on from that. And even if I had never made a penny from Insta, it had already changed my life. The positive feedback I got meant I forgot some of my insecurities in the other areas of my life because it made me appreciate the things I was actually good at. Then that positivity grew and started to influence other things. And that's the most important thing. So, find something you are good at, that you love – if you haven't already – and keep doing it. Get really bloody good at it! Maybe you'll find a way to turn it into a business, if that's what you want to do, and maybe you won't. But just by doing what you love and getting better at it you will get so much out of it – I can't think of a better way to get more confidence.

What would you do if you weren't scared?

Is there anything that you've wanted to do for a while but you just haven't? Sing karaoke? Learn to drive? Go on holiday by yourself?

Why is that? Try to be really honest about all the reasons. Money and time are often big ones, but it's true that we can also use things like that as an excuse. Are you scared of what other people might think? Nervous about making a commitment? Worried you might fail and have to deal with the disappointment? Really dig deep and figure it out, just in the privacy of your own head.

I would love to magic up enough confidence for you to do that thing and send it directly to your brain, but I can't. Maybe it will take you a while to get there, but if you can be honest about what's blocking you and then focus on imagining what it would feel like to finally do that thing and for it to go really well, I think you might find the door opens at least a crack. Perhaps just far enough that you can start wiggling through it.

❀ Don't be scared to try ❀

At first, I was so nervous about putting myself out there – I didn't think anyone would be interested and my mum and sister would see it and be like, what are you doing? And then the first time I was paid to make a video about something it felt really embarrassing. Iconic London sent me some mascara and blusher which I used for a few weeks and I really liked it. But when I looked on Insta all the girls who'd also posted videos were really glamorous and caked in make-up. I told Iconic London that I thought their products were great but I couldn't make a video where I piled on loads of make-up because it's just not me. They were totally fine with me doing something that was more about the natural look, so I recorded the ad and sent it to them and they approved it. I was really pleased as I'd never done an ad like that before.

But when I posted it, I had so many people message me to say, 'Charl, I just love you because you're putting the blusher in completely the wrong place!' I was putting it under my cheekbones and not on them, like, halfway down my face. I don't know how it got approved! It made me embarrassed, but it made me giggle, too. It was me to a tee though – I really liked the product, but I didn't have a clue about how to use it!

Over time, as I worked more with the company, I learned loads about how to put on make-up and I got really good at it. But it's like the first day in a new job when you don't know what you're doing and you probably are going to fuck up at some point. So, I did put myself out there, it went a little bit wrong and I did make myself look like a bit of a tit. And, yes, some people laughed. But that's because it was funny! I laughed at myself, the company still wanted to work with me, I learned more about make-up and hopefully I brightened up some of my followers' days when they saw me putting on blusher completely wrong.

It's like the first day in a new job when you don't know what you're doing and you probably are going to fuck up at some point.

If you never put yourself out there, you will never find out what you are capable of. You have to risk getting things wrong, or looking stupid, otherwise how can you learn new things or have new experiences? The person you ask out might turn you down. You could fall flat on your face in front of strangers on the dance floor. Shocking pink may turn out to be a terrible colour for a hallway. That could happen. Or maybe they'll say yes, you'll find out you're a great dancer and the hall will look amazing. Whichever way it goes, the world will keep turning and I promise you won't spontaneously combust in a fireball of embarrassment. (In reality, things are rarely that extreme, are they? That's just the way our panicked minds think – or maybe just my all-or-nothing BPD mind. Probably, the person you ask out will say yes, you'll have a few dates but they won't turn out to be the one. You'll have a fun night out dancing and the hall will look good, but you'll change your mind in a year and paint over it …!)

Most people are too wrapped up in their own insecurities to even notice what someone else is doing. Sure, there are people out there who, because they are unhappy in themselves, might want to try to knock you down. But you can't go around thinking that's everyone. Most people are nice and will cheer you on. Other people don't give a shit what you do and wouldn't even notice if you made an absolutely massive tit of yourself, so you can't let the idea of the mean minority, who are probably struggling with their own issues anyway, get in your way.

What's the worst that could happen? Really.

If you are someone who tends to always fear the worst, maybe there's a way to turn that into a positive thing and use it as a technique to help you go for something that you have been lacking the confidence to try. Ask yourself, what's the worst-case scenario if it doesn't work out? And how bad would that really be, in the long term? Try to be fairly realistic – it's not like the sky will fall in or you'll be on the ten o'clock news for being a twat! Most of us are worried about feeling embarrassed if we try something and it doesn't go well. But if we can get past that, then so many things become possible. Imagine it goes tits up and you tell your mates about it. Would anyone else even be interested that you tried something but fell on your arse? You might find that when you think about it, the worst that could happen isn't even that bad. It might just give you a really funny story to tell. So, knowing that, how about you get out of your own way and just go and do it?

Why do we care so much about what people think?

Why are we so bothered about other people's opinions anyway? I used to never wear shorts because I was embarrassed about my cellulite. My ex once made a comment about it and it really stuck with me. I thought if I wore shorts, everyone would be shocked at how my legs looked and they'd all talk about it. But then I realized no, they probably wouldn't, and even if they did, why do I care? If I'm walking through Cardiff and someone sees me and says to their mates, 'She's got cellulite' – if that even happened, so what? One, what actually is the issue with cellulite anyway? Who decided it's a bad thing? Two, you're never going to see that person again. And three, you never heard them say it so you'll never even know. You don't stare and talk about other people, do you? So, there's no reason to think every man and his dog is doing it to you.

When you really think about it, it's weird how much we care about other people's opinions (or the ones we just imagine they have) on some things even when we'd never be bothered about what they thought normally. If some random told me what curtains to buy or how I should bring up my kids, I wouldn't listen to a word of that. So why should I worry about what they think about the backs of my legs or a video I put up on Stories?

I know I'm probably making it sound easier than it is – it does take a long time and a bit of work to get to the point where you don't worry about other people's opinions, unless they are people you care about. But it is magic when you do. When you stop letting other people's opinions – or what you think their opinions might be but probably aren't – affect you, then you get that negativity out of your head and it makes room for confidence.

Don't get me wrong,
we all have our hang-ups.

It's hard not to care what people think because human beings are made like that. My confidence gets knocked all the time, but I don't have to let negativity take over. I'm definitely not saying it's the easiest thing in the world – it isn't. And making it sound like it's as easy as saying 'Be more confident!' is not helpful because then it's like when people say 'Love your body!' and it makes you feel worse because at the time, you just can't. Or, 'Be the

When you stop letting other people's opinions affect you, then you get that negativity out of your head and it makes room for confidence.

best version of you!' and you just think, *fuck off, today I am being a terrible version of me*. But if you just take one step over the line towards something you wouldn't have done before, even if it's just a tiny one, then that's half the battle because you've done it and that means you can do it again.

I turned the camera around and realized that people didn't just like my cleaning tips and my upcycling, they liked me, too. If I'd never tried and just worried about what they might think, then I never would have known. So, you have to take that first step. You don't know if something is going to be successful until you try it.

Some things won't be, true, but that's fine. Not being afraid to fail is one of the best superpowers there is.

What other people think of you is none of your business!

Caring too much about what other people think and letting that affect your choices is basically the opposite of 'you do you'. And so often we are just projecting our own fears and insecurities onto them and they're not even thinking about us at all! So if you find yourself obsessing about what other people think, try this:

- Focus on what you really care about. What's the bigger picture here?
- Let go of anything that isn't actually important. What someone who doesn't know you thinks of your choice of career/haircut/music taste is so far down the list of 'things I should care about' that it falls off the end, right?
- Remember, this is not a rehearsal – this is your life and it's the real thing! What will you be missing out on if you let the opinions of others get in your way?
- If anyone does criticize you, remember, it's more likely to be a reflection of how they feel about themselves than anything to do with you. And that's their problem, not yours.
- Ignore these people and find your cheerleaders. Remember, we should all be lifting each other up, not dragging each other down. So, if you need to, get the support of the people in your life who make you feel positive.

Remember, this is not a rehearsal – this is your life and it's the real thing! What will you be missing out on if you let the opinions of others get in your way?

Remember the times you were knocked down and got back up

After I left my ex and became a single mum, I learned so much about myself. When I finally got out of that relationship, I was so broken and I didn't know how I was going to get through it – I still don't know how I did it, really. I just kept putting one foot in front of the other and tried not to fall down. And sometimes that's all you can do. Not every day can be cupcakes and rainbows and positive freakin' affirmations, can it?!

If you've recently been through a tough time and you're still getting yourself back together, then I know from experience that your confidence has probably taken an absolute battering. All I can say is that I am sorry and I promise it will get easier. Just do what you need to do for now, let other people help you and hold on tight.

Let other people help you and hold on tight.

If you've been through something shit but managed to put it behind you and dust yourself down, then you probably know what I'm about to say. It is so often true that when something knocks you on your arse and you manage to get back up again, then you come out stronger from the experience. Don't get me wrong, I wouldn't wish it on anyone, but sometimes it is, weirdly,

Sometimes it is, weirdly, the shit times that bring you confidence in the long run because you think, *well, if I survived that, I can do anything.*

the shit times that bring you confidence in the long run because you think, *well, if I survived that, I can do anything*. It's like I always say, you can't change anything in your past, you can't undo what's been done, but everything that happens makes you who you are and you have to try to find a way to embrace that.

I think most of us are stronger than we think. The year 2019 was such an emotional year for me. It was heartbreaking watching my kids dealing with one of their parents suddenly being sent to prison and them not being old enough to understand why she wasn't around. I had to be everything to them – I taught Enzo how to ride his bike, I watched Brody as he had his first swimming lesson, knowing he was afraid of the water. I had to be Santa, the Easter bunny, the tooth fairy – and all while trying to pick up the pieces of my own life. But knowing that I did all that and that I'm now the happiest and most fulfilled I have ever been is such a source of strength for me.

You don't have to be Superwoman all the time

I'm not saying that we should throw a party for every horrible thing that comes along, though. No one can be strong all the time. The massive irony of the online world is that although I have been lifted up and made better by the amazing people who have messaged me to say they liked something I did or that I inspired them to create something of their own, there are of course others who have never met me, whose lives I have no bearing on whatsoever, who still feel the need to contact me and tell me what a shit person I am.

I'd be lying if I said the trolls don't get me down and knock my confidence sometimes. I try not to let them, of course, because I know in my head that they are probably not having a great time of it themselves – because why would you want to hit out at a stranger and try to make them feel shit if you were happy in yourself? But it can be hard. Imagine getting into bed at night, thinking, *today I went to work, renewed the car insurance and abused someone I don't know online* – who does that?

I love my job and I get to be so creative and do so many interesting things, but that doesn't make it easy to deal with abuse. You don't have an HR department in social media. If you worked in Tesco and you had someone coming up to your till every day, saying they thought you were stupid and you had a big forehead or whatever, someone would probably think it was their job to do something about it. You could talk to your manager or HR. But you can't do that

I love my job and I get to be so creative and do so many interesting things, but that doesn't make it easy to deal with abuse.

No one can go through life without a care in the world and you shouldn't feel like you have to pretend everything is going amazing when it's not. That's not what confidence means.

if you're on social media. A lot of people think you should suck it up, get a thicker skin. Or just get off social media altogether. Wouldn't it be better if the people slinging the abuse left? We don't think the bullies should be allowed to win in any other areas of life. It can all get pretty creepy too. People hide behind fake profiles and then message you to say that they've seen you on the school run or in Boots or something. They haven't, they're pretending because they want to play mind games, but a bit of you can't help but be freaked out all the same.

So, while I think knowing that you had the strength to get through the tough times can be an amazing and powerful thing, however confident you're feeling there will always be things that knock you. And that's OK. No one can go through life without a care in the world and you shouldn't feel like you have to pretend everything is going amazing when it's not. That's not what confidence means.

What are you actually really good at?

Right, I want you to think for a moment about all the things you're good at. List as many things as you can. Write them down in a notepad, make a list on your phone, take out an advert in the paper ... Anything that comes to mind, whether you're a really compassionate friend, or you make an amazing spaghetti bolognaise. Maybe you can run ten miles or you're a really supportive boss at work. Perhaps you're bloody good at putting up shelves. One of mine is that I can clap my bum cheeks – not everyone can do that, can they?! Write some of yours down here in the box below – I'll wait ...

Things I'm bloody brilliant at ...

You rock! So, own it.

I don't think most of us spend enough time thinking about what we're good at and appreciating our achievements, but we should, because it's a great source of confidence. If you're just naturally talented at something or you've been doing it so long you barely notice it any more, then you probably don't realize that other people are looking at you and wishing they could do what you do – or, even better, feeling inspired by your confidence to give something a go themselves.

Also, we're often told when we're younger that no one likes a show-off, that you shouldn't brag, and I think this means that as adults we can play down our achievements in case people think we're up ourselves. Girls in particular are taught to be 'modest'. I remember when I was little, my singing teacher told my dad that I was a really good singer and he replied, in front of me, 'Don't tell her that, she'll get too big for her boots.' I was so sad and I didn't sing after that because I thought it meant that my dad thought I was crap.

Young girls in particular need to see older women being confident.

Being confident and owning what you're good at, what you've achieved, is a good thing. Just like complimenting someone else on their achievements is, or helping those coming up behind you to do the things you've done. Young girls in particular need to see older women being confident and not batting away compliments like being good at something is embarrassing or something to be ashamed of.

But do you know what? If we get too big for our boots, why don't we just go and buy some bigger fucking boots?

Making a home for Enzo and Brody where they were safe and happy even though I had no money is something I'm proud of. Buying my own home was a big achievement for me. But so was making those curtain pole goals for my kids to play with on the day we moved into the old house.

It doesn't have to be a massive success to fill your heart – I'm very proud that I can clap my bum cheeks.

Everyone Deserves a Fresh Start

In the last chapter, I asked you to think about all the things you are good at, big or small. Now I want you to think about all the things you have in your life now that are great, that you love. Again, definitely include the big things, like, 'I have a bloody brilliant group of friends who are so loyal and a real laugh', but don't forget the smaller ones that give you a happiness hit. Like, 'I'm so glad I bought that plant pot for the patio. It looks fucking lush.'

Here, I want to talk a bit about starting over and about the things that we dream of doing, but I think it's really important that we always remind ourselves to appreciate the great stuff we have already. I believe that you can change anything if you want to, but the other side of that is that it can be all too easy to focus so much on the future and where you're headed that you don't give yourself enough credit for how far you've already come and what you have now. There might be areas of your life where you feel you are struggling or you're not there yet, but there will be other ones where you're killing it. Plus, some things seem to get more attention and more rounds of applause than others, and that's often down to other people's expectations rather than what we really want or feel inside.

So, I want you to remember two important things that might sound like they contradict each other, but they don't, they are just two sides of the same coin:

You are enough as you are.

AND

Don't be afraid to dream big.

You deserve good things.

♥ My fresh start ♥

My life changed so much for the better when I moved into the original Miss Greedy's Home. Because I didn't get on with my parents, I'd spent a lot of my early teens sleeping round at friends' houses and then when I was with my ex, we moved A LOT.

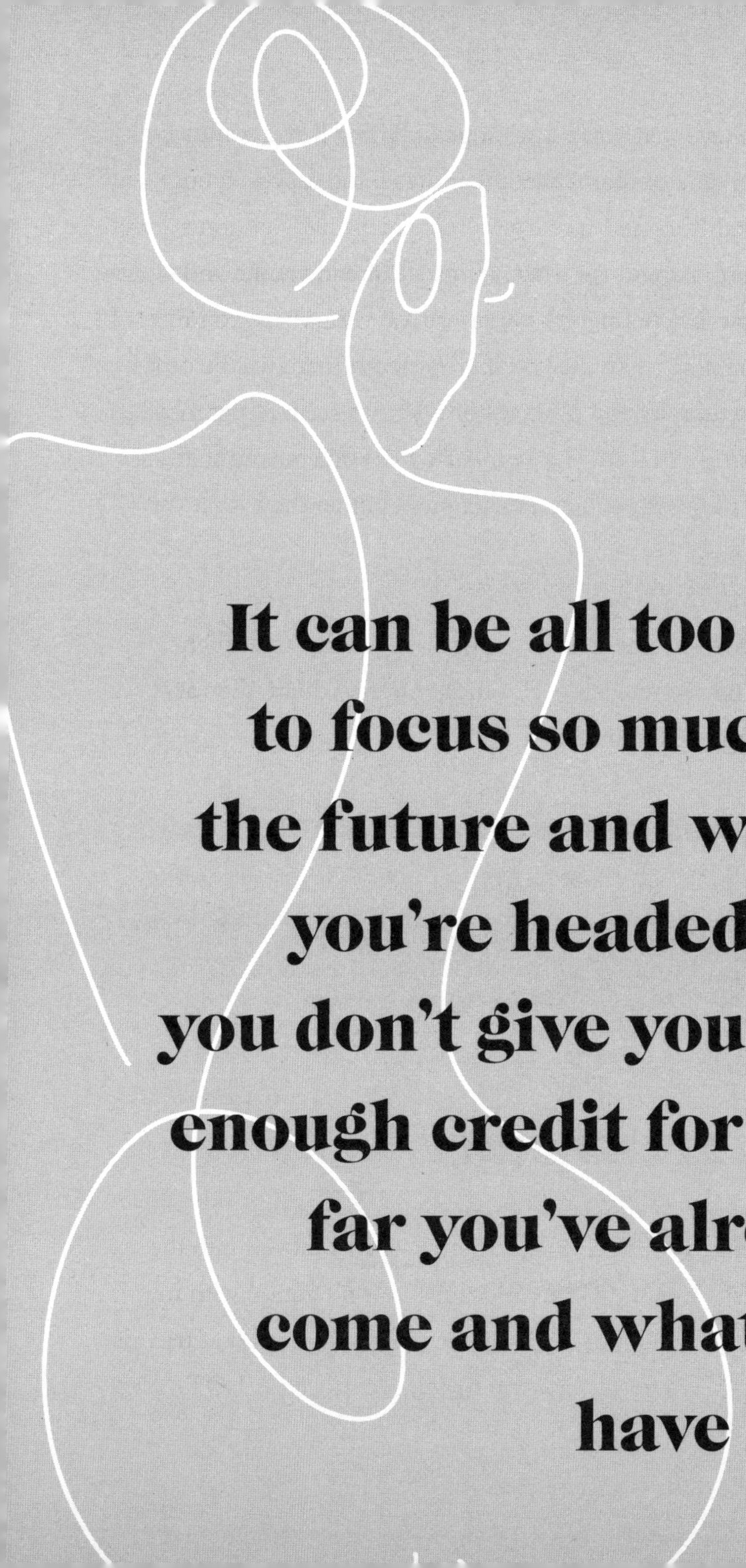

It can be all too easy to focus so much on the future and where you're headed that you don't give yourself enough credit for how far you've already come and what you have now.

It got to the point where we were moving every six months and it wasn't a stable environment for the kids.

The first big change was when I got our first council house: it was the first house in my name. That meant it was my responsibility to pay the bills and make the house a home for Enzo and Brody, but I felt so much safer and a weight lifted off my shoulders. Though you obviously still have to pay rent in a council house, if you are struggling they help you and don't just boot you out.

I felt so much safer and a weight lifted off my shoulders.

So, although it was when I managed to do that swap and we moved into Miss Greedy's Home that I got the fresh start that I needed so badly, there were a few baby steps I had to make first. I would love for you to have a home that you are proud of and that reflects you, your taste and the way you like to live your life, but I want to tell you that if that's not how it is for you

It's hard to be creative and to believe in your dreams if you are trapped somewhere you don't want to be.

right now, then you can get there. It's so hard when you don't feel like you are in control and everything seems overwhelming. I absolutely know in my bones what it's like. If this is you, then please be kind to yourself, firstly, and try to get to the heart of whatever it is that's wrong and think about what is in your power to do.

You can get there.

It's hard to be creative and to believe in your dreams if you are trapped somewhere you don't want to be – whether that's because of your mental health, a bad relationship, money worries or anything else that might be bringing you down. You will get your fresh start, but you might just have to start small and change a few things today and a few things tomorrow and keep trusting in yourself and your own abilities until you get there.

Talking about money

This is something we don't do enough, in my view. There is so much motivational talk online, about living your best life and seizing the day and whatever, and that is great and inspiring as far as it goes. But if you're struggling for money and you've somehow got to stretch out the cash and feed the kids until the end of the month then lighting a candle and doing some breathing exercises isn't going to be of much immediate, practical help, is it? I don't personally believe that chasing after money is the best route to

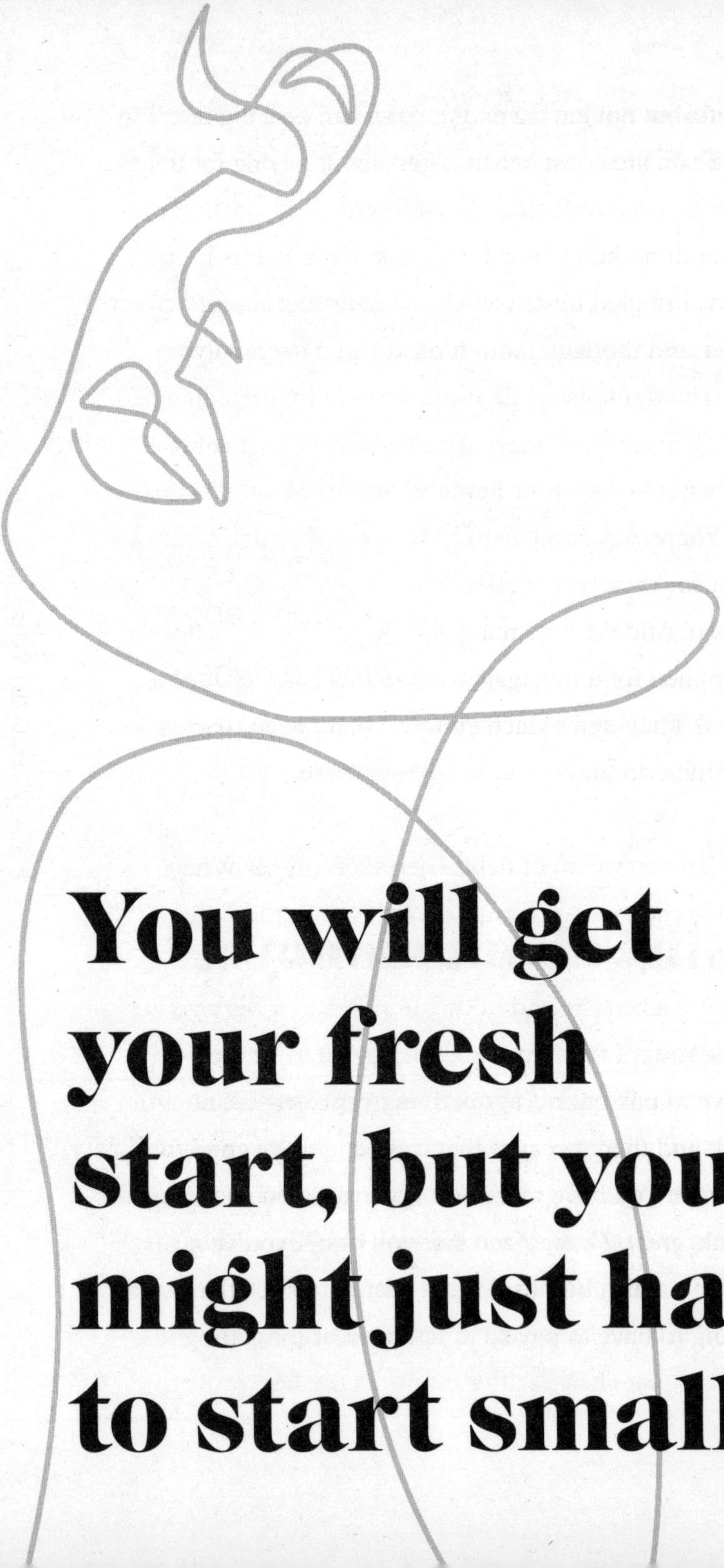

You will get your fresh start, but you might just have to start small.

happiness in life, but not having enough of it can be a big factor in how you feel, if you are constantly worried about paying for things.

Looking back, I don't know how I got by at some points in my life. In one way, I'm glad I was young and naive because if I'd been a bit older and thought about it more, then it probably would have terrified me! But I do think we're not taught enough about money when we're younger. Think about all that rubbish we learned at school – like, how many people in this country actually use a Bunsen burner for their work? Hardly anyone, I reckon. And yet how many people have applied for a mortgage or a credit card? They don't teach you about that, though, do they?

We're not taught enough about money when we're younger.

I was in over £10,000 worth of debt when I left my ex. When we were first together, we went out one day but we didn't have any money so I got a payday loan – they'd give me £100 and I could just pay it back at the end of the month. Being very young and an absolute mug, I thought it sounded great. And then of course you have to pay back £175 or something. It's insane. But you pay it back and then, because they've seen you're good for the money, they let you have more and it's costing you a fortune. You might think, *great, I have £200*, but you don't, you've got £25 or something really, because you've just paid back the last lot and you're going to have to pay so much interest for getting that money then.

The local bailiff was like Shrek and The Rock put into one man.

What with all the unpaid bills, we got to the point where we had bailiffs coming round the whole time. It takes a few years to really catch up with you when you start to get into debt, but then of course it does and it's constant. The local bailiff was like Shrek and The Rock put into one man. He was so scary; he'd come to the door when I was at home with Enzo on my own. I remember once the landlady was buying a new front door for the place we were living in and asked if I wanted one with windows or without and I didn't even need to think about it – I said, 'Without, please,' because I didn't want the bailiffs being able to see when I was at home.

I did eventually pay off all that debt and got a clean slate, but my God, it took ages! And now I'm so uncomfortable with owing any money because of how much negativity that debt brought me. I've never had a car on finance, or anything really. I always want to earn the money first to buy what I want and then I want to pay cash. I've only just now got a credit card! I do one shop on it a month and pay it off, but it still makes me feel a bit sick. If you have the sort of lifestyle where you have a regular wage and it makes more sense for you to get things on finance and pay them off, then I totally get it. The only thing is that it does tie you in and makes it a bit harder if you want to change jobs, you

I've only just now got a credit card!

want to take a short career break at any point or your situation changes because you're committed to lots of payments for a period of time. There are loads of people offering credit on all sorts of things these days, but you should always think really carefully before taking on debts and loans unless there is a good reason and you feel confident about paying it off, even if your circumstances were to change a bit. Do you really need this thing now or can you wait and save up for it?

But while I'm careful with money, I still believe in spending it on things that are really important to you. My dad has worked really hard his whole life and he is super-careful with money, but when my sister and I were young, we went on lots of lovely family holidays. That was a part of my childhood that was good. I remember we went on a cruise when I was about eight or nine and a parrot stood on my head – I'll never forget that! I'd never been that close to a parrot before, it was AMAZING! We were on this island and I saw them bringing a boatload of bananas up onto the beach. For some reason I assumed they were in a boat because they'd just got them out of the sea. For years, I thought that bananas grew in the sea! And I remember the water being so clear and finding these massive shells, like the ones in the film *Moana*. We don't get shells like that on Barry Island! It's the experiences that stay with you and even

But while I'm careful with money, I still believe in spending it on things that are really important to you.

though my childhood wasn't great, those trips meant, and still mean, a lot to me.

Now I want to make the most of my time with the kids while they're young and take them away when I can so they get to have some interesting experiences and understand a bit more about the world. And yes, you have to have money to be able to do stuff like that, but for me personally, I do think that's a good thing to spend it on. Better than just buying the kids more stuff. I think people think Harriet and I go away a lot and it does make me really happy to take the boys to different places, whether that's Trecco Bay, thirty minutes down the road, or we go abroad, it doesn't really matter. I spend most of our wages on holidays because I think that's what the boys will remember. But that's just me. I get that some people really like to stay home. You do you!

I still think I can't afford posh bread.

If you're constantly living on the edge of your overdraft, then I hear you. For years I had a £750 overdraft and I was always close to reaching the limit of it. It's a relief that we don't have to go to Tesco any more and put the butter back. I still think I can't afford posh bread, though! I try to be open about finances with the kids – as far as is appropriate for how old they are – because I want them to grow up with a realistic understanding of money and not make the mistakes I did. But of course, Enzo's eight so he's constantly asking, 'Can I have this?', 'Can I have that?' So yeah, it's not working yet! But then Enzo is a saver – he will save all his pocket money and not spend any of it! I've explained to him that it's OK to spend it on something that you'd really like, when you've saved and you've thought about what you want. We have more money than we did when Brody started school and I was doing a bit of cleaning and working in a pub at the weekend. But I don't want Enzo to think that we've got a load of money and that happiness is all about having showy things. Because it's not.

It's the time you spend,
not the money you spend.

At the moment, Enzo is determined to be a policeman or a binman when he grows up. Whatever he says that he wants to do when he's bigger, I'm like, 'Great! That would be brilliant.' If I'd have said that when I was little, my dad would have told me that I couldn't be a binman because I was a girl and that binmen don't get paid enough. But why does a kid need to hear that? You're just shutting doors in their faces. Let them say what they want and don't start telling them things aren't for them. It's not like he's going to walk straight out of Year 4 and go down the council offices expecting to be handed a promising career in collecting people's rubbish.

My dad tried to drum it into us that we had to get a really good job because otherwise we wouldn't be able to live properly. He

I don't think money should be this big taboo subject and definitely not how we define ourselves or our success.

made me think that if I didn't study and get the same results as my sister I wouldn't be able to afford beans on toast, even. It didn't help because it made me really confused about money and anyway, as usual, I went and did the opposite!

As you can see, I'm the last person in the world to be giving anyone financial advice, but I don't think money should be this big taboo subject and definitely not how we define ourselves or our success. I want my boys to understand it so they can make the right decisions, but I hope they never think it's the be-all and end-all and if someone makes more money, they are better than them.

The problem with five-year plans

I'm going to tell you something you won't find shocking – I'm not much of a planner. I think we all need our dreams and to know that we have the power to go after them; that we deserve to go after them. But I also think life can be complicated and getting obsessed with mapping out the next five years of your life can set you up for failure and make you so focused on a few stages and goals that you forget to appreciate what you have now. It's almost like you're saying to yourself, 'Everything will be great *when* …' at this point in the far-off future, when actually I bet there's a lot that's great about now.

Having a really specific plan and following it to the letter can also mean that you just keep going after it because you once made that decision, even if things change and it might not be the right decision for you any more. It's fine to change your mind about things. We're constantly learning and growing, and different people come in and out of our lives. That can mean our priorities change. So being too wedded to this idea you've always had in your head might blind you to new things and different paths.

It's fine to change your mind about things.

We will all go through times when everything feels like a huge effort and it's just about surviving and getting through the day. That's me when my mental health is bad, or in the time just after I split from my ex. At these points, thinking about the future can seem scary and overwhelming. The last thing you want to be doing then is torturing yourself that you don't have a series of goals and some master plan for where you want to be in five years. In those days, weeks, months, focus on what you can do and just keep going as best you can.

Make plans when you are ready.

But what if you don't know what it is that you want?

If you're reading this and thinking, *actually, I do want to make a five-year plan because that's how I think and that's right for me*, then go for it. You do you. But what if you don't even know what you want yet? That's fine and totally normal. I don't think most people start to know who they are and what they want to do until they're in their mid-twenties, or even later. You don't have to know it all and have it all sorted. If you're trying to figure it all out, make some time to really think about what makes you happy. If you can put yourself in a good place and think positively, then you will be able to trust your instincts.

Here are some questions that might help. Change them around as much as you need to so they are relevant to you:

- What makes your heart sing? What do you love to do more than anything else?
- What could you never compromise on?
- What would your ideal working day look like?
- What would be your perfect weekend?
- What experiences would you like to have in the future?

- What would you like to learn to do? Big things and little things, they all count.
- When you are really old, looking back on your life, what would you be most happy to be able to say about it?

I know some of these are pretty big questions, but give them some thought and write down your answers. Then come back to them in six months or a year and see if anything has changed. I think knowing what you want to do in life and making good decisions always, always starts with knowing yourself.

When you're ready to make a change

Change is exciting, but it's also scary. People say that all the time because it's true. But it's never too late to do something different and start on another path. It's not always easy, especially when you're a bit older and you have responsibilities. I obviously had my kids really young and that impacted on what I could do and the decisions I could make. But I built a life for myself off of just being myself and finding something I was good at. And if I can do it, you can too.

If I can do it, you can too.

Knowing what you want to do in life and making good decisions always, always starts with knowing yourself.

My friend is a hairdresser. She did an apprenticeship, worked her way up and became a salon manager. What she really wanted to do was be a police officer, but her dad, who is a police officer, was always against it because he said he didn't want that life for her. And you can understand his point of view of course, because he knew what it was like and she was young. But now she's doing it: she's completely changing her job and becoming a police officer. I think that's amazing, I'm really proud of her.

If what you want to change is your job, then that can be hard because starting over in something different often means taking a pay cut while you get established in the new career. For some people, that's going to be challenging. If your partner or someone else is able to support you for a short time while you make a change, then go for it. If you can afford to reduce your hours at work while you get some experience in your new area, then do that. Think about what you need to make it happen and who can help you. If there's an opportunity there and you have figured out how it would work, then don't second-guess it. Ask yourself, *would I regret this if I don't do it?* If the answer's yes, then you should probably go for it.

Amazing things almost never happen overnight, but there's a world of possibilities out there. You just have to sit down and think about HOW you can make what you want happen and be prepared to work for it.

It's fine to feel scared. Fear is there to protect us, to stop us getting hurt. But sometimes you just have to have a word with your inner self and say, *thank you for warning me about the risks, but I've got this and I have just got to go for it.* Though maybe do that when you're by yourself so your family don't think you've lost the plot.

When you get what you want

There are a million motivational quotes that you can print out and put on your wall, stick on a Post-it or write on your forehead if you want. Do all of that if it helps, though what a lot of people don't talk about is that the path you are on is not always going to be smooth. Sometimes you can get what you want and it's not how you thought it would be, or it feels different to how you thought it would.

The path you are on is not always going to be smooth.

When I'd cleared my debts and – I couldn't believe it – I was still making money, H and I realized that we didn't need to be in a council house any more. We could afford to buy our own place. We found the house we are now in and it was like a dream. When we moved in, the first weekend, I was just walking around gobsmacked. The first time the mortgage came out of the bank

If fear is holding you back ...

If you're someone who worries, then dig deep and look at it from all angles. Feeling like you've got a proper plan and you've covered all the bases may make you feel more confident and secure in taking a leap and going after what you want ...

- Make a proper plan in terms of money, time and your responsibilities. When are you going to start? What's the first step?
- Who might you need help from? Have you spoken to them about it? It's harder for people to be supportive if they don't know what's going on! And if you're going to need help with childcare or anything like that, then you might want to set that up in advance.
- What's your back-up plan if it turns out not to be the right thing for you? At least then if it doesn't go the way you hoped, you'll know that you really thought about it and you won't be left panicking about what to do next.

account I was really excited! (Even though debt usually scares me.) I must be the only person who was delighted to be paying a mortgage. I was like, *that money's gone from the account because I'm paying for* my *house!* I just couldn't believe it had come true.

Now, I know this could well come across as ungrateful, but I'm going to tell you anyway because it's important to be honest. Once we'd been in there a little while I started to feel a bit sad and I missed the old place, the original Miss Greedy's Home. That was mine and the boys' home, my safe place. It was the first place I'd lived where I never shut off any of the memories because all of the memories we made there were good. Nothing was bad there. I'd been so wrapped up in the excitement that I didn't acknowledge that I was taking a big step. I'd thought that our old house was going to be our forever home and it took time to say goodbye. I couldn't stop thinking about the doorframe with the kids' heights marked up it as they grew – I should have cut it out of the wall and brought it with us.

I felt guilty because the new house was everything I'd dreamed of and I'd barely thought of anything else while we were in the process of buying it. And I was so lucky to be in that position – how could I feel sad and miss the old place? But I just needed to accept that was how I felt. We have complicated feelings about things sometimes and it doesn't help to pretend we don't. It doesn't make me spoilt or selfish, it's just the way it is.

Of course I love the new house and I'm proud of everything I have achieved to get us here. At first, I found the amount there is to do overwhelming but I've started making progress now and getting stuck into some projects has really helped. Which just goes to show that at times when you feel uncertain it's good to go back to what you love, what you're good at and the core things that make you, you.

I hope you get your fresh start, you achieve your dream, and it's everything you hoped it would be. But I wanted to tell you about this (even though I might be coming across as an ungrateful twat – hopefully not!) to show that it's OK if you have a wobble sometimes. We can't always know how we're going to feel about something until it happens.

It's OK if you have a wobble sometimes.

If you want to give up, remember who's watching

I haven't always felt strong or motivated so I know what that's like. I've made mistakes and messed things up and I've said nasty things that I didn't mean. I still have days when I struggle to get out of bed, even though I now have so much in my life that I love and that I'm proud of. So, I want you to know that I'm proud of you whatever you manage to do. Please don't ever give up. If you're feeling shit or something hasn't turned out the way you'd hoped, please don't just lie in bed thinking about all the things you can't face and instead decide what you think you can do. Even if that's just getting up and having a shower, it's a start.

When I was back in the old house, struggling to put myself back together, knowing in my heart that the most important thing in the world to me was making a home for my beautiful boys kept me going: they were watching and I couldn't let them down. So, find whatever that thing is for you. That core truth that you can come back to, that reminds you why you're doing what you're doing.

You might have kids or a partner who you love and who you want to be a good person for. That's great if you do, but if you don't, that doesn't matter. Because the person who you are ultimately doing it all for, the person who is watching, is YOU. You only have one life and you deserve for it to be amazing, whatever that means for you. Nothing less.

> I spent a lot of time trying to prove other people wrong, but now I'm trying to please myself.

I've told you about my stubbornness and, as I'm sure you've guessed, it's not always a good thing! In fact, it's often a pain in the arse. I'm bad at saying sorry, for one. I'll basically whisper it and once I've said it, I don't want to say it again! But it's

You only have one life and you deserve for it to be amazing, whatever that means for you. Nothing less.

also true that it got me through a lot of tough times, especially when I was younger. When it felt like no one thought I would amount to much, when my ex thought I would never leave her because I couldn't cope on my own, that drive to dig my heels in and prove everyone wrong was useful. I spent a lot of time trying to prove other people wrong, but now I'm trying to please myself.

If people are saying you can't do something, you can use that as fuel. That's fine. But this is one of the most important things I have learned: ultimately, it has to be about not proving that they are wrong, but that you are right. It's not about showing someone that you could do something they said you couldn't but showing yourself what you are capable of. If you focus on proving someone wrong, you are focusing on them.

Focus on YOU.

It's like I said before, how can other people's opinions of you be more important than your own? They can't, they're not. All of that energy we spend on worrying about what other people think, measuring ourselves by their standards, is energy wasted. If you can use that to figure out what you want, what makes you happy and how to get it, then I promise it's so much better. Love and value the good people in your life and let them help you when you need it. And lift them up when they need you there. But know that whatever is the right path for you is the right path. Life is tough and it's a rollercoaster. If you take only one thing away from reading this book, I would love it to be remembering to be kind to yourself.

You are the one who carries you through life and you need to take care of you. You deserve to be happy just as much as anyone else. If no one has told you lately then I will: I am SO PROUD of you. You are AMAZING!

YOU DO YOU!

Write Yourself a Letter...

I'm not someone who usually writes stuff down and I know that I could be better at stopping and reflecting sometimes. I'm not great at letting things out of my head, I've never done therapy or anything like that. Writing this book is the first time I've properly thought about some of the things that have happened to me – and it's been a wild ride!

It's really shown me that, particularly if you're the sort of person who lives in the moment, or you find it hard to talk and to let things out, it is so, so good sometimes just to stop and appreciate how far you've come.

The person you were got you through so much; you should thank them for where you're standing today.

No matter what mistakes they might have made, you owe them everything for making you who you are. And the person you're going to be in future is going to be incredible, too. So, if you feel like you want to, reach out to them. Write them a letter. I know it sounds cheesy as hell, but you might just find it helps you appreciate all the things that have made you, you. It definitely helped me. And, like I have here, why don't you write a letter to future you as well? I think it'll be so fun to read this back when I'm older and it's good to give yourself an opportunity to get excited for all your dreams for the future.

A letter to my younger self

I always wanted to end this book with a letter to my younger self and one to me in the future. But every time I've sat down to write this in the past few months I've shut the book and walked away. I guess I was trying to completely ignore it, if I'm honest. Before I started writing *You Do You*, I thought I was OK with everything from my past, but it has brought back so many memories, so much hurt, pain, sadness, but also so much happiness, all at once. Which is *so* confusing.

But this is it – I'm doing it, this is finally my closure.

The first thing I want to say to my younger self is: Charlotte, I am so proud of you. I am so fucking proud of you now, you as a teenager and you as a young kid. I am proud of every single thing you pulled yourself through, of the amount of shit you put up with and coped with by yourself. You were always told by different people – teachers, parents, peers and in past relationships – that the way you handled things wasn't acceptable or right, but they absolutely were. For you, they were.

You were feisty, passionate and fierce when you knew something was right and you never gave up on yourself. You may have felt completely broken and worthless at times, but you never once gave up. You didn't realize it back then, but I can see it now: that strength and determination is incredible and you deserve proper credit for it. You dug your way out of some pretty shit situations all by yourself. You were at times mistreated and completely misunderstood, you were always underestimated, but you never once gave up, even when you wanted to.

In the end, you proved every single person that ever doubted you wrong. And THAT I'm proud of.

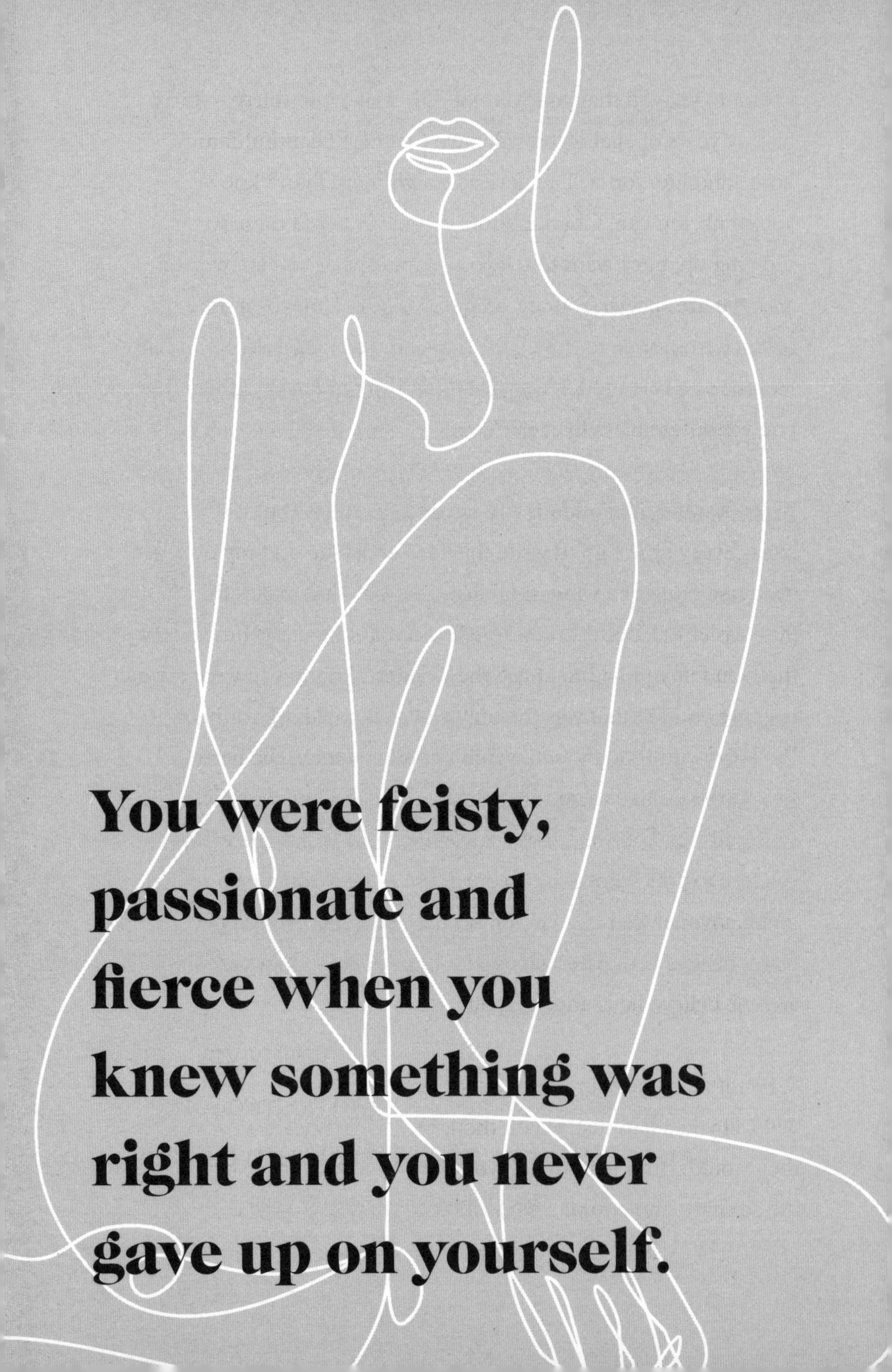

You were feisty, passionate and fierce when you knew something was right and you never gave up on yourself.

I want to tell you that you will not only make it to thirty – thirty bloody years of age! – you will have the most beautiful family, home and life. You will achieve so much more than I know you think you can. Charl, I know you never heard these words growing up, but I want to tell you so much that you are worthy and you are special. You are unique, if – OK – maybe a little off balance from time to time! I wish you, my teenage self, could have had me as a role model in your life, as I would have told you that you are nothing less than perfect.

There's something else I really need to say to you but it's really hard. Every time I go to write this bit I choke up and my eyes get heavy, so I've got a wine in my hand now as that makes this bit a little easier to let out! I want to tell you that I'm sorry. I'm so sorry that you felt you had to abuse the wonderful body you were given because you felt that was the only way you could ask for help. I'm sorry you thought you weren't good enough to be here and I'm sorry you had to go through so much pain on your own. It's so unfair that you were taken advantage of by someone who was so close to you, who abused your trust. I know you are so scared to tell anyone what is going on because you are terrified people won't believe you. After all, you idolize this man, so why would anyone believe he is abusing you?

I'm sorry you had to go through so much pain on your own.

When it all comes out, some people will call you a liar, just as you thought they would. But I want to tell you that the strength and courage you will find to finally stand up for yourself, to not be backed into a corner to change your story, is something that will make you into the woman you will become. I'm sorry you feel like you are nothing and I'm sorry you are convinced that what happened in those few months is your fault: it wasn't. NONE of it is your fault. Part of me wishes I could somehow go back in time, like a guardian angel, and protect you from all that. But, as I now know and have said throughout this book, the things that happen to you, good or bad, are what make you into a strong, kind, fiery and passionate woman.

You, Past Me, moulded me into who I am today and I'm sitting here with the biggest glass of wine to say cheers to YOU for not just standing up for yourself but for standing up for what's right. I hope that if there is someone reading this who is in a similar situation to the one you were in – too scared to tell anyone because they'd be called a liar – that they can find the courage to stand up for themselves, too. I'm proud of you for using your voice back then and I'm proud I have told the story now, too.

I've told you I'm proud of you and I've said I'm sorry for the things you had to go through. So, I'll end my letter with thank you – thank you for getting me to where I am today and thank you for never, ever giving up. You have made me a strong, independent, determined young woman who thrives off achieving the 'unachievable'. I'm an incredible mother to my two boys, a good partner

Thank you for never, ever giving up.

to my H because of you and a good friend to a handful of special people in my life – because of YOU. Who'd have thought it, hey? Who'd have thought I'd be sitting here in my beautiful home with my beautiful fiancée, my two wonderful children, dogs Kobe and Minnie, cat Beau-Beau, living my absolute best life writing MY BOOK for people to read. The odds were always stacked against us, girl, but we defied all those odds.

Actually, there is one last thing to say:

I LOVE YOU.

I love you and your perfectly imperfect body. The scars you made are beautiful. I know you hated them for so long but I want you to know that I love them now, those tiger stripes you created on our journey to here.

Cheers to you, Charl – cheers to all that you are, all that you were, and all that's yet to come.

xxx

A letter to my older self

Now, I'm not one to look too much into the future because, as we all know, I live for the moment and putting loads of specific plans in place to map out the years to come is just not my style. Living life for now is just me all over, but a letter to my older self is something I thought could be fun. I've come a long way and I'm in a good place right now, so maybe future me will like to be reminded of this time. Or, at the very least, it'll be something to look back on when I'm in an old people's home!

So, future Charl, I hope if you're reading this at forty, fifty or sixty-plus years of age, you're sitting there with a glass of wine in one hand and a box of Guylians in the other! I hope your boys are visiting you lots and maybe by now you've even got a few grandchildren around your feet. I hope you are sitting outside your bungalow by the sea, the one that H and I talked about last week while walking the dogs. And I definitely want you to still be flirting and winding H up!

I do hope you're not still trying to get that bloody 16-year-old body back – the one that I'm still, currently, promising myself is going to happen! I reckon you've figured out by now that it's absolutely not. I think you've probably realized that you love wine, pizza and chocolate seashells way too much! Either way, I hope you have learned to be completely happy and content in your body and ditched the yo-yo dieting for good, as that's what I'm trying to teach myself now. Don't get me wrong, I'd love to read this back in the future, having actually completed Couch to 5k at least once to the end, mind, instead of giving up after week three, haha! But lesbi-honest, you and I both know that I'm never going to be that athlete I keep promising myself I'm going to be!

I think you've probably realized that you love wine, pizza and chocolate seashells way too much!

The only goal I have right now is to be loved by H when I'm old and wrinkly and to have the best relationship with my children, who don't feel it's a chore to come and see me. So, I hope you, future Charl, have really nice daughters- or sons-in-law and you haven't turned into a monster-in-law, LOL! One of my worries about being older is that the kids' partners might hate me, so if you're reading this and they're round for dinner every Sunday, well bloody done you! Goal achieved! (If you haven't achieved it, then go pour yourself a larger glass of wine and shut the fekkin' book!)

The only goal I have right now is to be loved by H when I'm old and wrinkly.

I'd like to think you're still doing your skincare regime every morning and evening. I also like to imagine you're still doing stories on Instagram, dancing! (Imagine me at fifty or sixty, dancing around my bedroom, making my bed, still spraying Febreze on it every morning, while wearing the latest version of Crocs! OMG!)

I hope you're beaming light to everyone around you.

On a serious note, I hope you've found a balance in your life and that you're taking care of yourself. I'd love to know that you're still on a self-care journey and that you love yourself more and more each day. I hope you're beaming light to everyone around you, that helps inspire them to be themselves and to fully exist. I hope you have inspired more and more people than you had already at thirty and that you have learned to be a little (just a little) less hot-headed. Have you managed to pull a few more of those walls down? (Only a few, not too many, mind, but enough so you have a good few friends around you.) I hope you're waking up each morning excited and happy to be alive, finding ways to spend your days filled with things that bring you joy. And that you're able to 'be bored' a little more. You'll remember how 30-year-old you felt guilty for being bored, so I hope you've learned to enjoy doing nothing sometimes.

I just know you'll still be humble but never crumble under pressure. And that you're still investing in memories and moments, not things. Lastly,

I hope you've learned to enjoy doing nothing sometimes.

I hope you're standing on that hill you built yourself, looking around at the roots from which you grew to be who you are and living with no regrets. Oh, and I really, really do hope H let you have those ten golden retrievers when you retired. If not, there's still time to change your mind about her. (Just kidding!)

I hope you're in a better place mentally and you're the happiest you could possibly be. You deserve to be.

Yours sincerely,

Thirty-year-old you xxx

Thank You

My first thank-you goes to you, my followers reading my book. You have changed my and my family's lives by simply following a journey I accidentally took on social media and I'll never ever be able to say thank you enough. Thank you so much for continuing to follow my path in life and buying a book you all so badly wanted me to write – I'm so grateful for every single one of you.

The biggest thank-you goes to my wonderful friend and manager, Alan Samuel at Spotlight Management, who is not only an absolute angel at managing me but also a forever friend who I cherish and adore so much (you owe me some chilli cheese bites from McDonald's for that!) :)

A massive thank-you to Lauren Gardner, who put all my messy ideas from my head into a structured deck to help me get a book deal. Without her, this book wouldn't exist.

An even bigger thank-you to the wonderful and beautiful Kate Fox at Transworld (Penguin Random House) for believing in all my messy ideas and having as much excitement as me about this book. You really did make me smile from ear to ear in our first meeting and I'll forever remember your wonderful smile and enthusiasm. That meant so, so much to me when picking a publisher, thank you :')

Liz Marvin – you are such a wonderful soul and I cannot thank you enough for bringing my vision for this book to life, spending hours and hours, which definitely felt like days and days, talking to me. Taking all my ideas in, listening to my life story and getting it all on paper is such a talent. I'm in awe of you and your work and my book wouldn't be what it is without you. (PS Thanks for the therapy. LOL :)

Thank you to my Mamma Bear, for not just being my mother but my best friend too. We have the best relationship now and I love you millions and millions.

To my amazing cousin Jade and my Auntie Julie, two of the strongest women I know, who look out for me and look after me when I struggle, even when they have so much going on themselves. You are two of the most important people in my life and I love you both so, so much.

Thank you to Rodders, my best friend in the whole wide world since we were thirteen. You have been through hell and back with me and we have been through the same life experiences as each other. You're the bestest friend a girl could ever wish for and I really wouldn't be here today if it wasn't for you picking me up and dragging me through hell, time and time again. Thank you for always being there, for always giving the worst advice and always getting me into trouble, and thank you for making me see my worth, thank you for helping me through the hardest time of my life and making sure I didn't go back to someone who treated me so badly. I wouldn't be me today without you – love you too much!

Thank you to H, my wonderful partner who has picked up every single piece of me when I've been at my worst, believed in me when I haven't and joined this crazy journey with me. You have been one of the biggest parts of this journey and I cannot thank you enough or love you any damn harder. I believe true love meets you in your mess and not your best. When someone sticks around no matter how hard things get, they really love you. Thank you for loving me so unconditionally. (And thank you for holding the fort at home and keeping the kids alive while I wrote this book – I honestly couldn't have done it without you! :)

And lastly, thank you to my wonderful boys, Enzo and Brody, who have made me who I am today. They have given me the best job in being their mother and I hope I'm making them as proud of them as they make me. One day, a few years ago, I decided to turn our life on its head and make a fresh start – for us, for ME. For me to be a happier mummy for them. It was the best decision I have ever made, but without them looking up to me, I'd never have done any of this. I am SO proud of you both and I couldn't love you any more if I tried :)